NORTHWEST PIONEER

illustrated by Morton Garchik

NORTHWEST PIONEER

✠✠✠✠✠✠✠✠✠ *the story of Louis Fleischner*

by Alfred Apsler ✠✠✠✠

Farrar, Straus and Cudahy *Jewish Publication Society*

82.9H

To Robert and Ruby Apsler,
born in the Pacific Northwest,
whose parents came to this land
from the same land as the hero
of this story.

Alfred Apsler has also published (in collaboration
with Rabbi Julius J. Nodel) *The Ties Between:
A Century of Judaism on America's Last Frontier*

CONTENTS

You have never heard of Louis Fleischner? Well, don't feel embarrassed. Few people have, outside his immediate hunting grounds in the Pacific Northwest. Though very colorful and reasonably successful, he was, after all, only an average man, not counted among the great ones of history. Yet there is reason to make him the hero of a story. First, his life was adventurous and beset with dangers and hardships. And secondly, he is singled out here as the representative of a whole group which richly deserves to be better known and appreciated: the Jewish pioneers who, almost one hundred years ago, helped settle and civilize an empty country. A little band of simple, yet courageous young men, they shared the trials and the joys of frontier life with brave men of many religions and races.

Louis Fleischner was a real person, perhaps the most fascinating one among the immigrants from Central Europe who found their way to America's last frontier. He roamed the forests of what is today Oregon, Washington, and Idaho. He was a friend and companion to gold miners, Indians, homesteaders, and packers. Not all of the events described in this volume involved him personally, but they were part of his time and his environment, and if they did not occur to him, his friends and associates figured in them.

Since there exists hardly any printed source material, my information was gleaned from many interviews with old-timers and the descendants of pioneers, from browsing through old letters and newspaper clippings. Especially generous with time and information were Mrs. Henry J. Berkowitz, a grand-niece of Louis Fleischner, and also Mrs. Irvin Trachtenberg and Dr. M. Monte Bettman, all of Portland. I am indebted to Rabbi Julius J. Nodel, former minister, and Mrs. Elsa Voremberg, former executive secretary of Temple Beth Israel, who made it possible for me to use the archives and old record books of the congregation. Grateful acknowledgment should also go to the personnel of the Oregon Historical Society, the Oregon State Library, and the Portland and Vancouver Public Libraries.

My two children deserve a vote of thanks for having read the manuscript and criticized it from the point of view of the type of reader for which it is intended.

A. A.

🌲🌲🌲🌲🌲🌲 *Last night at home*

An air of excitement filled the synagogue of Vogelsang, a small town in Bohemia. The prayer hall was
nothing but a large bare room. From its tiny windows one could look out on the steep-gabled houses
which formed the crooked "Jew Street." On the
Sabbath morning of eighteen forty-four the hard,
straight-backed pews were well filled. Several men
stood on the center platform wrapped in long prayer
shawls bending over an open Torah scroll. The
reader was reciting the weekly portion in a high-
pitched singsong.

During the long reading many eyes strayed from
the printed copies of the Bible and looked at a
slender boy in the first row. He fidgeted while his
father beside him patted his thin shoulders re-
assuringly.

From behind the curtain that enclosed the women's section came a steady buzz of talk. In vain Reb Wolf, the old sexton, sent outraged glances in the direction of the curtain. Even when he rapped loudly on the lectern and bellowed, "Quiet there," the talk ceased only for a few seconds. There was too much on everybody's mind.

"Poor Sarah Fleischner," whispered a rather stout lady, wiping her forehead with a silk handkerchief. "This is the first time in years she's missed *shul* on a Sabbath. She is really sick with grief."

Several women around her nodded.

"I know how I would feel," added her neighbor, "if my child were to leave tomorrow for the other end of the world."

"She didn't want to let him go," said a voice directly behind them. "The boy kept on pleading with her till she consented. Well, at least he's taking the trip to America with relatives. His two uncles from Bavaria are meeting him in Hamburg."

"America, America," grumbled an elderly woman, "Everybody's talking about America, especially the children. I tell you it's that new teacher that puts all the crazy ideas into their heads, that they'll have more opportunities there, that we are old-fashioned and that we are also poor."

An older girl came to the teacher's defense. Her cheeks were flushed:

"Reb Sh'muel's a fine man and so good with the

children. He believes America is the best country for the Jews."

The old woman was not satisfied. "You might think the streets there are paved with gold," she said.

"Hush," broke in the stout lady, her nose pressed against the curtain. "Levi Fleischner's walking to the platform. They're calling him up to the Torah for the last time. My, what a handsome boy! And so tall for only fifteen years."

Not a sound came from the women's section till young Levi had chanted the closing benediction. Then the old rabbi, his usually strong voice shaking with emotion, blessed the boy.

It was some time before the group behind the curtain dared to relax.

"The poor darling," said an old woman. "This is not like going to Prague, the capital city, or even to Vienna where the Emperor lives. America's a barbaric country. The animals are wild and the people are even wilder."

She shook her head in disgust. "Who has ever heard of a Jewish boy going to live with red Indians?"

"If you want to know, Frau Bauer," said an attractive matron, "the Fleischners are doing the right thing. Sarah may cry her heart out now, but she will never regret it."

"Bah, a child belongs with father and mother. He shouldn't run off into the wilderness."

"But look what Levi can expect here in Bohemia. Soon he will be mustered into the Austrian army, and you know how Jewish boys are treated there. And the boys know, too. The older brothers and friends have told them that the officers give them fewer privileges and push them around. When they get out of the army they are forced to return to this cramped Jew Street because they are not allowed to live anywhere else. They can't even get married unless their fathers bribe some greedy official or other into giving his permission. These are stern laws and they are no secret."

"That's bad enough," said a woman in the back row, "but on top of it all, you never know how long you will be allowed to stay in your own home and earn a living. At the first sign of any kind of trouble, they drive out the Jews. We've seen it happen time and again."

A general whisper of agreement followed these sad words.

"I wish my Moses were old enough," said a young mother. "I'd send him to America even though he's all I have. As long as Napoleon ruled over all these lands, we were treated like human beings, but now—"

"Sh, careful" a frightened voice whispered. "That sort of talk's dangerous. The walls have ears, even in *shul*."

At that moment the congregation rose to its feet

as the *chazzan* lifted the Torah scroll high. Chanting solemnly, he led a small procession around the reading stand and then carried his precious burden back to the Ark. With undivided attention, men and women followed the final part of the Sabbath service.

The echo of the last *kaddish* had barely died when the crowd spilled hurriedly into the street. It felt good to be outdoors again under the mild spring sun. No flowers or shrubs could grow on the gray cobblestones. From far beyond the heavy iron chain that barred the entrance to Jew Street, the dark green forests of the Sudeten Mountains greeted them. The children began to run happily up and down the street while the grownups chatted in small groups.

Levi came out, walking between his father and his eleven-year-old brother Jacob. Levi seemed tired. In his Sabbath clothes he looked older than his years. But young Jacob was enjoying the attention being given to his family.

From all sides hands were extended to wish Levi good speed. It seemed as though everyone had a word for him.

"Don't trust a fellow unless you know him well. America's full of dangerous outlaws."

"Write and tell us whether tailors or watchmakers are needed in America."

"When you begin to pick up money dig a good deep hole to hide it in."

"Find my nephew if you can," the sexton asked

him. "Remember, he left a few years ago from a southern German town. I've heard that he's now made his way to Philadelphia."

At the outer edge of the crowd, a young girl was standing, with blond braids peering from below a neat blue coif.

"Come, Hannah," her mother urged. "Won't you say goodbye to Levi?"

The girl clung to her mother as if she were afraid to move.

"Now Hannah, don't be foolish. He's your neighbor, after all. You've played together most of your lives, though I must say that in the last two years it's been more fighting and teasing than anything else."

Gently she pushed Hannah toward the center of the group. The girl looked downward, her cheeks crimson.

As small children they had been inseparable. Then, one day, Levi came to the conclusion that she was only a girl, unable to share in the rough adventures of the boy. Then he avoided her and she felt left out and humiliated. But a few months ago, the arguing between the two had ceased. Whenever they met, they only exchanged a few awkward words, vaguely embarrassed.

Now Hannah was standing in front of the neighbor boy and the crowd closed in behind her.

"Goodbye, Levi," she whispered. "Take good care of yourself."

" 'Bye, Hannah. Perhaps I'll see you in America."

He wanted to say more, but with all the people staring at them the words would not come. He felt a strange new tenderness toward her.

Their fingers barely touched as they shook hands, and then she rushed away to hide her tears. Curious glances followed her. Some older people exchanged knowing smiles.

2

Jacob was already sleeping peacefully that night when Levi slipped into bed beside him. The last night at home. The garret room was crammed with all the treasures collected by two growing boys. He could not see them in the darkness, but he knew they were there. The room was quiet, but the sounds of shuffling feet and muffled voices still came from below.

He lay awake for a long time. Tomorrow he would sit in the rumbling stage beside old Yan, the red-nosed coachman. He would change coaches several times. Hamburg, the big port city, was far away.

Jacob's elbow poked into his ribs. The younger

brother was probably fighting a dream battle with the boys from the next street.

Where will I be sleeping a year from now? Levi asked himself. Of course, he had been away from home before. He used to go to school in Tachau, not far from here. Tachau was a little larger than Vogelsang and had a high school, a *gymnasium*. Then he had visited Pilsen a few times, a bustling city of fine shops and markets, and once the family traveled to the famous watering resort of Marienbad. Then, too, his father, who was a horse and cattle dealer, had often taken the boy on his visits to the peasants in the villages. But that had all been different. From every adventure he had returned to his own bed and to Mother's delicious strudels which nobody else could bake so well.

Yes, he would be lonely out there across the Atlantic. Nobody would be waiting to meet him. He was the first boy from western Bohemia to venture so far.

Dimly the moon outlined a row of black leather-bound books on the dresser.

He would miss Reb Sh'muel, the kindly teacher in the Hebrew day school. Reb Sh'muel never used a strap on the children as his predecessor had done, and they all loved him. Often when they had recited their Bible lesson well, he would tell them about America where people were free to practice their religion. In the gaunt teacher's eyes was a gleam as he told them how, in the darkest hour, God always provided new lands where the bravest of His children could find rest from persecution. Once troubled masses of Jews reached a haven in Spain, then in Holland, in Poland; and now America invited them to build a new life.

"I would set out for the New World myself," Reb Sh'muel used to say, "if I were stronger and healthier. But it is rugged people with stout hearts who are needed there."

Levi had always felt that such words were especially addressed to him. Even after he had outgrown the *heder*, he often visited its teacher and they took long walks together. The frail man had to stop frequently when his coughing spells seized him, and Levi waited patiently till he could go on. The man spoke to the boy of the German and English language books he read during the night. The books told of the fur traders, of the Liberty Bell and the American Constitution. They described brand new cities where there were no Jew Streets.

Levi stared at the darkened ceiling. What dangers would he have to face on the other side of the ocean? He thought of all the warnings he had received during the last weeks. But he was not afraid of danger. He wanted excitement, a chance to look into the unknown, and the right to carry his head high.

Sleep came at long last.

3

It seemed to Levi that he had only just closed his eyes when a gentle hand shook his shoulders. The first gray of dawn was coming through the attic window and his father's face was close. The elder Fleischner's voice was soft and caressing:

"Time to get up, Lev. Yan won't wait if you're not ready. He promised me to stop at the house. Come, get your *tefillin*."

Levi dressed in silence, careful not to wake his brother. Together father and son turned toward the east and recited the morning prayers as they had done every day since Levi's *bar mitzva* two years ago. Then the man placed his hands on the boy's head and blessed him. He took one pair of the leather phylacteries, the prayerbook, and the short silver-trimmed prayer shawl and stuffed them into a blue velvet bag. "Here," he said, pressing the bag into Levi's hand. "Don't lose it. This will remind you of your God and of your home."

The larger and the smaller hand met for a moment. Both trembled slightly. Then father and son went downstairs.

Sarah Fleischner smiled bravely under her red swollen eyes. It was obvious that she had not slept all night. She heaped brown potato pancakes and sour cream on the breakfast plate.

"Eat, my Lev, eat. Who will make pancakes for you in the cowboy country? Promise me again, my darling, that you will be very, very careful, for my sake."

Levi only nibbled at the food though this was his favorite dish. His usually strong appetite was gone, and there was an uneasiness in the pit of his stomach. He felt relieved when the clatter of hoofs could be heard outside. There was a sharp report, like a shot. But it was only Yan's whip. He always had to show how expertly he could swing it.

In spite of the early hour, a small group of neighbors surrounded the coach. Levi's father was working hard to fit the bulging carpetbag under the carriage seat while his mother clutched an enormous package from which rose the scent of freshly baked delicacies.

"Here, take it along, Lev, my child. May God keep you."

In spite of all her good intentions, she broke down and sobbed uncontrollably.

"Now, now, Mama." The young hand reached out through the open window to pat her tear-streaked cheeks. "Don't fret. I'll be back, I promise. You and Father and Jake will all come to America with me, and we'll all be free and happy. You'll see."

Again Yan cracked his whip. The horses snorted

and off they went. In another moment the short cavalcade had rounded the corner of Jew Street and was out of sight.

Nobody noticed a small girl's face crowned by a blond wisp of hair that was pressed flat against an upstairs window of the neighboring house. Two big tears rolled down her cheeks and dropped on the windowsill.

✤✤✤✤✤ *Restless blood*

It was eight years later. Night had come early and the March air was chilly. Across the prairie whistled an unfriendly wind. A few log cabins poorly chinked with plaster made up the hamlet of Drakesville in southeastern Iowa, a way station on the dusty Old Alexander Trail on which pioneers traveled westward from New York and Pennsylvania.

One of the cabins had a rickety porch cluttered with barrels, crates, and cords of rope. Above the confusion hung a weather-beaten sign announcing in uneven letters, FLEISCHNER BROS.—GENERAL MERCHANDISE. A good-sized corral behind the roadside store held horses and oxen.

Inside the cabin it was comfortably warm. The front room which served as the store was crammed with a hundred and one things: flour and sugar in large bags, spices and coffee beans in tin boxes, nails and screws in wooden barrels. Heaped on the counter were tools, books, calendars, and spools of thread. Rough outdoor clothes hung from nails along the walls.

There was no one in the store at the moment, but from the back room came the sound of laughter and the clatter of dishes.

Two young men were sitting at dinner. The table and benches were of rough-hewn lumber, but there was a white tablecloth and the glow of candles made the room look festive. Thick slices of meat were heaped on the plates. The men dipped the brown gravy with chunks of fresh home-baked bread.

A large Negro woman with a kindly face appeared from the kitchen carrying a platter full of triangular cookies.

"Look, Louis," shouted the younger of the two men. "This is Sally's idea of *Hamantaschen*. Not quite the way Mother used to make them in Vogelsang, but close enough."

He took a piece from the platter and helped himself to a hearty bite.

"Sally, they taste like heaven. And you must be one of the angels. To think that you had only my poor directions to go by. It's a miracle."

The housekeeper beamed with pride as she listened to the exaggerated praise.

"I'm sure happy you like them, Mister Jacob.

Now what d'you call this festival you're celebratin' tonight?"

"It's Purim. On this night we remember how, a long time ago, a brave woman named Esther freed the Jews of Persia from grave danger. It's a feast of joy and thanksgiving."

"The folks down in Alabama sure could use an Esther these days," sighed the woman. She carried the empty platter back into the kitchen. The brothers were left alone.

Again it was the younger man who spoke up:

"What ails you, Louis? You haven't said a word since she brought the dessert. Is this the way to behave on Purim? It's a time for merrymaking, not for brooding."

Louis did not even hear what his brother was saying.

"No use talking to you when you get into that mood," grumbled Jacob. "Might as well step out and have a look at the corral."

2

Louis' mind had wandered back to the last Purim at home. The children had dressed up in rags and old clothes from Grandmother's trunk. They had paraded through the streets, singing and shouting.

From open windows people threw candy and coins at them, much to the distress of the little band of musicians who also made the round of the houses. The fiddlers and bass players feared there would not be enough left for them.

Then came the first Purim in the New World. Timidly the lonesome boy rang the bell of a stately brownstone house. A wealthy Sephardic family lived there. They were goodhearted, but proud people, always mindful that their ancestors had been the earliest Jewish inhabitants of America. Louis was grateful for the invitation, but he felt uncomfortable throughout the long evening. They did not mean to make the poor newcomer feel inferior, but they could not help it. He never came back to their house.

Those were years of hard work. Like other boys who had recently come from Bohemia or Germany, Louis tramped through the countryside, a heavy peddler's pack on his shoulders. Then he hired himself out to a merchant who, like his father, bought and sold horses and cattle. Many nights he found himself too tired to eat or even to sleep. Yet he enjoyed riding up and down the Delaware Valley. It was thrilling to discover new landmarks and to make new friends among the men.

In the presence of younger women, however, he was still as shy as he had been when he was a boy.

3

Louis' mind, trained in the study of Hebrew grammar, quickly learned English. Slowly his loneliness dropped away as his conversations with the plowmen and the stockmen of the valley became longer and livelier. Of course, he spoke with a foreign accent, but so did many others. This was the country of the newcomers.

He was proud of his own name, Levi. But his employer took to calling him Louis. The customers learned it from the horse dealer, and the English name stuck to the boy. Only in the synagogue was he still Levi, the son of Sh'Lomo.

Still lost in his reveries, Louis turned his head so that his eyes focused on the tiny window. On the low hills campfires glowed under clusters of elm trees. The Fox Indians had pitched their tepees again. They were gathering for the annual hunting expedition.

This was a good country. Louis remembered how he had grown here from a slender youth into a broad-shouldered man who walked with firm steps. Yet he was still restless, and as he traveled about on his business he met many others who were also impatient. They had come to America to seek adventure, not to settle down to steady living.

To the west lay an unknown world, empty spaces beyond imagination. One could only dream of the treasures that lay in the wilderness waiting for those bold enough to go out and search.

Around the pot-bellied stoves of stores and taverns, young men talked about the frontier where the richest land could be had for the asking. Everybody could live there according to his own taste. No old-timers would look down their dignified noses at the latest arrivals.

As he looked out now, Louis could see the tents of emigrants from the window. The trail-sore wanderers had stopped here for a few days of rest. They were bound for Council Bluffs on the Missouri River where the long wagon trains assembled for the trip to the Far West. Iowa, only yesterday the farthest outpost, had become a way station into the land of gold.

Gold! Through Louis' mind flashed the memory of the day when the news arrived: gold had been found on Sutter's farm in California. The mad rush was on! The adventurers of two continents were on the move!

The young cattle salesman knew by then that he could not resist. He was itching to be off on the westward trail. But first he had to take care of a very important matter.

4

One wintry morning Louis stood shivering on the dock of New York harbor. He watched the gray mist till he saw the outlines of a ship materialize. Its deck was crowded with waving and shouting immigrants. When the gangplank was finally lowered to the pier, the mass of brand new Americans pushed and scrambled down, hampered by their countless bundles and boxes. Among the last to leave the boat was a pale young man, his eyes red with the fatigue of an uncomfortable journey.

"Hi, Jake, this way," shouted Louis.

An hour later the brothers were sitting in their simple hostelry. Their first conversation lasted deep into the night, and many more followed in the next days as they tried to relive together the years of separation. Not only the family, but everybody on Jew Street had read the eagerly awaited letters from America. Each message contained a plea to have Jacob follow in his brother's steps. Their mother fought hard to keep at least one of the boys at home. Jacob was still so young, she said. There would be lots of time later.

Then the ship's ticket had arrived; Louis had saved the money for it penny by penny. At last Mother gave in. Deep inside she had known all the time that no mother had the right to hold her children back in the stifling air of the ghetto. But when her second son left, she cried even harder than on that other day seven years ago.

Louis allowed his brother only a few months for a glimpse into the new life. Then they started out westward. With a group of land-hungry travelers, they crossed the Mississippi. The caravan disbanded west of the river, and the Fleischner boys found themselves in the sparsely settled Iowa Territory. Tiny frontier communities had sprung up here and there.

Before the brothers could make up their minds what to do next, they were besieged with requests to open up a store among the new homesteaders.

"You boys have the experience," they were told many times, "and we need you desperately."

The farmers and sheepmen of Drakesville had to buy tools and staple goods; their crops and animals had to be shipped to markets. The neighbors also wanted a place where they could meet and find out what went on in the great wide world.

Louis and Jacob felt flattered. Let the gold mines wait a while. Perhaps this was the Promised Land of their dreams. And so the crude sign went up over the little cabin.

5

Only the stump of one little candle kept the room from being totally dark. The sun had set a long time ago, but red still colored the sky outside.

The figures of men and women could be seen milling about the tents on the hillside. What were they expecting to find on the far side of this empty continent? Was it only gold with which to buy merriment and gay clothes? Or was there something more enduring?

Louis wondered.

When Jacob came back from the corral and found his brother still in the same position in which he had left him, he gave him a friendly slap on the arm.

"Come on, Louis. Enough of the dreaming. You know, I'm worried about you. It seems to me I've seen that look on your face before. Does it mean you're thinking of moving on?"

"And why not? Lots of fine people are joining the wagon trains. We'd be in good company."

"I might have known it. You won't be happy as long as there are empty spaces left. When we were boys on our hiking trips in the Sudeten Mountains, you always wanted to push on farther and farther. I wonder where the Fleischners got that pioneer spirit."

"Perhaps we're the first Fleischners who have the chance."

"A Jew and a pioneer: strange how the two go together."

"What's so strange about it? Jews ought to be pioneers. Abraham was a rugged pioneer if there ever was one; crossed the desert without wagons, and he didn't have a rifle to shoot himself some juicy buffalo steak."

He looked into his brother's eyes.

"Jake, you want to know what my dream was about? I saw a beautiful city by the Pacific Ocean, and I saw you and me riding through the streets. Everybody was shouting greetings at us, and we were waving back. It was *our* city, a city we had helped to build. We didn't have to shrink into corners and try to keep out of sight as we did in the Old Country. I saw our children romp around happily, feeling that they were at home—"

"Children, did you say?"

It was the gruff voice of the colored housekeeper. Returning to put the clean silverware back on the cupboard, she had overheard the last words.

"You're big ones to talk about children. If everyone behaved like you two, there wouldn't be any children. Why don't you fellows get married? You, Mister Louis, especially. When my George was your age, we already had four young'uns."

"All right, all right, Sally," laughed Jacob. "Just be patient."

"Getting married," said Louis after Sally had retreated into the kitchen. "As if I were not thinking of it all the time. Every day I want to write to Hannah."

Jacob became uneasy. He dreaded this, but Louis went on:

"When I think of my future home, I think of Hannah. I couldn't even imagine anybody else as my wife."

"Then why don't you ask her to come? How long do you expect her to wait?"

"I want her to have a real home. On the west coast I'll settle down for good. Then I'll send for her—if she'll still have me, that is. Do you think she'll wait for me?"

Jacob was about to give a grim answer. He wanted to warn his brother. After all, Louis had never made it clear to Hannah in so many words that he wanted her for his wife. Perhaps in his mind it was all settled. He had asked his parents to find out what she thought of being an American pioneer woman. But there had not been a direct answer, at least not while Jacob was still in Vogelsang. She might not even remember any longer what Louis looked like.

But Jacob could not bring himself to destroy his brother's dream. For Louis she would always be the little blond girl, gentle and sweet, and so obviously full of admiration for the tall neighbor boy.

Jacob was still trying to make up his mind what to say when the bell by the outside door began to ring. It dangled from the ceiling so that the door would hit it every time it was opened.

"Come, Louis," he said, relieved. "We have customers."

One of the neighbors, a young homesteader, had come in for an after-dinner chat. Soon others followed. The store filled up with men sitting on cracker barrels or leaning against sacks of feed. The smoke from corncob pipes lay over the gathering.

Several of the men who had broken the long westward trip here were about ready for the next lap of the journey.

"We've got an early spring," said the homesteader. "Won't be long till planting time."

"No plow for me this year," said the man sitting on the next barrel. "I'll be working with the rifle shooting buffalo."

"It ought to be a good buffalo season, but watch out for the Indians. They don't like the wagon trains running over their hunting grounds."

They exchanged opinions on buffaloes and Indians. Then the talk shifted to Rocky Mountain passes and to the scouts who guided the caravans across them.

"Hey, Louis," shouted one of the pipe smokers.

"Can you get me a prospecting outfit? Pick, shovel, sluice pan, and all the other stuff? I'm off to Sacramento as soon as I get the gear together."

"Sorry, we're all out of shovels and pans. Too many customers. Everybody's going after Sutter's gold."

"Blast it. How long do I have to wait?"

"Hard to tell. A shipment from the East should've been here long ago."

While the frustrated prospector snorted in disgust, Louis turned to a deeply tanned man with the rough hands of a farmer:

"What about you, Jeremy? You bound for California gold too?"

"Not me. We're taking the northern route, the Oregon Trail."

"You won't get rich in a hurry there."

"That's not what I'm after. I want a home for my family, a quiet place where the children can grow up straight and where the neighbors are friendly."

"Sounds inviting. You think you'll find all this in Oregon?"

"So I'm told. I hear the peaches grow better in the Willamette Valley than anywhere. And the streams are full of fat trout and salmon."

"You make it sound wonderful. But aren't you getting ahead of yourself? Right now it's still wild country. No roads, no towns, only bears, suspicious Indians, and a few wily Britishers who want no Yankee competitors."

"Sure, I know all that. Now listen to me, brother. Oregon's no place for people who scare easily. But just let a few more wagon trains of real men show up there, and they can make it God's country."

The traveler had become quite excited. Jacob and several visitors grinned in amused disbelief, but Louis looked at him with admiration.

"Who'll be the caravan leader this spring?" he finally asked.

"It's Ezra Meeker, one of the real mountain men."

His enthusiasm for Meeker was shared by several others. The name seemed to be well known.

"Ezra's been to Oregon and back several times," said an older pioneer. "What he doesn't know about the trail isn't worth knowing."

"I saw Ezra only yesterday," reported Jeremy. "He's camping somewhere 'round here. He wants to stock up. Then he goes to Council Bluffs to organize the caravan."

"I've met Ezra," said Louis. "He was here this morning to talk about some pack horses. Only he didn't say he was the leader of the Oregon-bound train."

"Do you want to see him again?" asked Jeremy eagerly. "I know his campsite."

"He'll come back to the store tomorrow to pick up a few things he ordered. I'll have a talk with him then."

"Why, Louis," broke in his brother in mock surprise. "This time the fever got ahold of you pretty fast. You're not thinking of leaving with the next wagon train? What about the store?"

"If we go, we might as well get under way. This Oregon sounds good to me. The store is in fine shape, isn't it?"

"In excellent shape. What with all the emigrants stopping by, it's made a good profit lately."

"Then we won't have to worry about a buyer. Perhaps we can trade it for a prairie schooner and the gear that goes inside it. We'll keep the horses and the oxen. You coming along, Jake?"

"Just try leaving me behind. Wouldn't it be a shame to break up the team when things begin to look really interesting?"

"I'd hoped you'd stick by me. But I haven't any right to drag you with me all over America just because I'm restless."

"It's all right. I'll ride with you for a while longer. But do you realize we'll be the first Jews on the Oregon Trail?"

"We'll show them that Jews make good trail-blazers."

"I wish they could see us now in Vogelsang." Jacob's eyes shone. "The two Fleischner boys from Jew Street going to the Pacific Ocean in a covered wagon."

He rubbed his hands together like somebody who is ready for action.

"Come on, Louis. If it's all decided, we might as well get to work."

The older brother turned to the men that filled the store:

"Excuse us now, fellows. Ezra'll be pushing on to Council Bluffs in a few days, and we want to be there when he fires the starting gun."

🌲🌲🌲🌲🌲🌲 *On the trail*

The men crowded around the fire. They did not want to miss a single word of the trail captain's final instructions:

"This is the plan, men. Tomorrow we're moving out. The platoon leaders 'll wake you up an hour before daybreak. Be quick with breakfast and hitching up. When you hear a rifle shot, swing your wagon into line according to your number. Tomorrow's lead wagon 'll be the last on the day after. Number two 'll take the lead, and so on. Keep in line at all times. Any questions?"

A bearded man raised his hand. From his stiff collar and black frock coat, one could guess that he had once been a teacher or an official of some kind.

"Mister, mein Herr, I, ich—" He stammered and

fought for words. Finally he let loose with a little speech in German.

"Can anybody understand what he wants? It's getting so a trail boss needs a squad of interpreters."

"He wants to know where he can buy food after today," shouted Louis Fleischner.

"Tell him at Fort Laramie, a few months from now, if he's lucky. Meantime he'll have to buy his meat with a rifle. Well, better get a few hours of sleep, all of you."

The Fleischner wagon brought up the rear on the first day out from Council Bluffs. There was shouting and singing. Women and children, decked out in their Sunday best, waved from under the flapping canvas tops while the men rode ahead on sleek prancing horses.

At Fort Kearney they joined up with emigrants who had come by way of Independence, another famous gathering place of the overland caravans.

Now the real adventure began. Strung out in a line, almost a mile long, the eighty-odd wagons lumbered along the shallow Platte River. The prairie was flat as far as the eye could see, but there was plenty of grass. Occasional clumps of trees relieved the monotony.

While the vehicles moved slowly ahead, impatient horsemen fanned out in search of game. Louis loved to gallop after the buffalo, losing himself completely in the thrill of the chase. He was now a splendid marksman, and often it was his rifle that made the final kill.

After weeks of travel, the grass became scantier and the night air cooler. Gradually the train worked its way up toward the headwaters. They crossed the Rocky Mountains at South Pass and then descended in a northwesterly direction.

The most dreaded part of the journey began when they reached the Snake River Valley in Idaho. Countless wheels and hoofs had worn deep ruts into the soil. Jacob worried about the unhealthy gray color of his brother's dust-caked cheeks while Louis looked with growing anxiety at Jacob's eyes, which the constant irritation had turned into a flaming red.

The August sun beat mercilessly on the blue-gray desert. For days it was impossible to descend the canyon and reach the cool water on the bottom. The trail was now lined with rusty iron stoves, with oak chests and bedsteads abandoned by earlier travelers to lighten their loads. The skeletons of draft animals bleached in the sun. More than once the wagons passed a shallow grave. Unevenly scrawled letters on a marker bore the name of a pioneer woman or child for whom the trail had been too long.

But the caravan moved on, covering fifteen to seventeen miles on an average day. Every afternoon when the rays of the sun had lost a little of their sting, the bugle sounded the call for rest. While the platoon captains shouted their orders, the wagons drew up in a large circle. Oxen were unyoked and all the animals were turned out to pasture. The first watch took up its position. There would be three more before daybreak, and the men were divided into three companies for guard duty. Each company watched one night and had the next two off.

Soon countless fires dotted the campground. The smell of frying meat drifted over the countryside. Around a fiddler a group of young people had gathered to sing a sad cowboy ballad.

2

The Fleischner brothers sat by their fire near the wagon. Louis' face was haggard and pale; his eyes had sunk deeply into their sockets. Jacob, though thin and parched, was as good-humored as ever.

"It's wonderful to see you out in the open again," he said. "For a while I was afraid I'd never get you off that mattress alive. It just proves once more that the Fleischners are a tough lot. Even cholera can't get them down."

The convalescent man managed a thin smile while he sipped the hot broth which Jacob had poured from a battered frying pan into his cup.

Company came while they were eating. Some men strolled over to witness Louis' recovery from the dreaded illness that found so many victims on this journey. They were a noisy, unkempt lot, but loyal to their friends and always willing to share dangers, as well as joys.

"Hey, Louis, you old faker," shouted a bearded fellow who wore a tattered buckskin jacket. "So you finally decided to mingle with the common people again. You coming out on the second watch with me tonight? Our company's on duty."

"I had a close call, Jess, and you know it, you big old grouch. But even if I were healthy, I'd have to disappoint you. This is the Jewish Sabbath. Ezra has it all arranged for us. If our watch falls on a Friday, we trade off with a couple of fellows from Company C."

"Sure, sure. Just slipped my mind. Kinda strange, though, to have Jewish boys along on the Trail. Yep, emigrant life is full of surprises."

"And what's wrong with Jews on the Trail? Don't we do our share of the work: the watches, the hunting, the Indian fighting?"

"Don't get sore. I meant no harm. Out here it doesn't matter where you come from, only that you do your part and the others can count on you when we get into a tight spot."

"The Fleischner boys 're all right," added another

of the visitors. "Remember how Jake shot that sneaking Indian horse thief down in Bear Valley the other night? That was some fun."

For the first time Jacob's face clouded. His voice sounded grim:

"Better not remind me of that. I know I had to do it, but there's something terribly wrong with the way we treat the Indians."

"The redskin's not human," said a whiskered pioneer. "Vermin must be stamped out before it bites you."

"Nobody whom God has shaped in His image is vermin. Yes, they raid and steal. But just try to treat them decently, and they'll act like human beings. I'm a Jew and I have an idea of what goes on in the minds of hunted people. That's one of the reasons I'm here."

In the meantime Ezra Meeker, the pilot of the caravan, had quietly joined the group.

"Maybe you got something there," he now said slowly. "Often when I lie sleepless on my blanket, I think about Indians. They have a right to be here. We're the intruders. And yet, there seems little else we can do but fight them."

His deeply creased face reflected the glow of the fire. Something was bothering the old scout. "You say," he continued after a pause, "they treat Jews in Europe like we do Indians. Then why, for heaven's sake, don't you strike back? At least the red man fights when he's cornered."

"And a lot of chance he has," explained Jacob. "The odds against the Jews of Europe are even heavier. The only solution is to pull out and go where we're accepted as equals."

"You got into the right company here, boys," answered the mountain man. "Still, I can't get over it. This is my fourth overland trip, and you're the first Jews who felt like coming along. The others I met in the East didn't look to me like they would enjoy sleeping by a campfire and being chewed up by mosquitoes."

He scratched his neck vigorously and waved his arms in a vain effort to discourage the tormentors hovering in thick clouds over the camp.

Louis' cheeks had lost some of their paleness during the debate. His voice was still a little unsteady:

"Just because the few Jews you knew were city dwellers, you think we're not fit for frontier life. Don't you know? Our people became shopkeepers and moneylenders not because they wanted to, but because there was nothing else for them to do."

"I suppose so. But whatever the reason, the Oregon country will never attract more than a handful of Jews."

"How about a bet, Ezra? I say that in my lifetime and in yours there will be large synagogues in the

Northwest, and the people of my faith will fill them. If I invite you to the consecration of the first one, will you drop everything and come to be my guest?"

"It's a deal, Louis. A Jewish church in the wild timber country: that I have to see before I'll believe it. I tell you what I'll do: if you win, I'll not only come to your first service, but you'll get my best deer rifle, the one I've had from my earliest beaver trapping days. Let's shake on it. All you men be witnesses."

Bets were always welcome additions to the evening program. The trail companions nodded. The deal was now valid, but all felt that the odds were heavily in favor of their leader.

Meeker looked up to the full moon. Slowly he emptied his pipe into the fire.

"Now we better call it a day. We must get out of this awful Snake Valley as fast as we can. Tomorrow we break camp at the usual time, Sabbath or no Sabbath. So long, boys."

"Good night, fellows," called Louis as the group dispersed. Then, moving closer to the glowing embers and unrolling his woolen blanket, he turned to his brother. "Good Shabbos, Jake, and good night."

3

The wanderers were shivering under the first chills of autumn when the wagons entered the magnificent Grand Ronde Valley in eastern Oregon. The slopes were tinted blue from the petals of the camass plant. Graceful elk looked up from their leisurely meal and then darted back into the dark forest, full of disgust.

On that evening a dignified delegation of Nez Percé warriors rode up to the protective corral. They were a superior tribe of Indians: clean, intelligent and sociable. To the guards they handed gifts of jerked venison and beaded leather moccasins. As it was obvious that the visitors meant no harm, they were invited inside the wagon enclosure. Soon some lively bartering was in progress.

Like most of the emigrants, the Fleischners were devoted swappers. With the help of sign language and a curious mixture of Indian, English, and French words, they tried to outdo the others in acquiring valued articles. This was one of the few forms of entertainment available on the trip.

It was not long till Louis was tying a well-fed Indian pony to his wagon, which he had traded for his old trail-sore horse and a sharp hunting knife with decorated handle. The new owner of the knife was immediately surrounded by his admiring tribesmen. It had been a good bargain for both parties.

The last leg of the journey led through extremely rough country. Many wagons broke down and had to be abandoned in the gullies of the Blue Mountains, but finally the train emerged from the thick pine forest onto softly rolling hills. The purplish hue of sagebrush stretched endlessly in all directions. Otherwise the land was barren.

It was late in the morning, and the sun had almost reached its peak. Eagerly children and grownups were awaiting the signal for the short noon break.

The group of horsemen that rode ahead of the lead wagon had just reached the crown of a bluff. Suddenly they stopped, bringing the whole long line to an unscheduled halt. Soon people on foot and on horseback were swarming forward to find out what had happened. A sudden stop often meant trouble.

But this time it was different. As Louis and Jacob reached the top, panting for breath, a picture unfolded before their eyes which they had longed to see for months.

"The Columbia River," they shouted. Gray-haired men jumped like children. They shrieked and laughed and pummeled each other's backs. Without shame they wiped tears from their cheeks.

Below stretched the mighty river of the Pacific Northwest, steel-blue under the spotless sky. On the bank several plumes of smoke hung over stone chimneys. That was The Dalles, the town which marked the end of the trail. It was good to see real houses again, though they were no more than ramshackle cabins.

There were boats on the river. In a few days, the new arrivals would be sitting on top of their bundles, floating downstream on long rafts, singing to each other across the water. Waiting farther to the west were the sites of their new homes.

For a long time Jacob looked out over the river. Then he turned to his brother:

"If Father were here with us, he'd say that old blessing he always kept for really important moments. Do you remember it? My Hebrew isn't as good as it used to be back in the *heder*."

"I know what you mean." Louis' eyes swept over the panorama of mountains, water and sky. Slowly he spoke the words:

"*Boruch atto Adonoy Elohenu Melech ho'olom shehecheyonu v'kiymonu v'higiionu lazman hazzeh.*

"Blessed art Thou, O Lord our God, King of the Universe, Who has kept us alive and sustained us and brought us to this moment."

✟✟✟✟✟ *Warpath*

The brand new northwesterners were camped on the north bank of the Columbia near the mouth of the Willamette River, except for several families that had already left to take possession of their land claims. On a gentle morning when a fine steam was rising from the damp meadow, the two brothers from Bohemia said goodbye to their companions of the Trail.

A large group surrounded the wagon which had been reassembled after the raft trip through the river gorge.

"Take good care of yourselves," called Meeker. "Come to visit me soon. The latchstring on my door is always out."

"We'll be over your way," answered Jacob from the driver's seat, "as soon as the roof is up and the land is plowed."

A young woman held a baby, one of several that had been born on the Trail. With her free hand she grasped Jacob's extended right hand.

"Don't forget us," she shouted. "Let's have a big get-together of all our caravan folks after the first crop's in."

There were more such promises and invitations. Many voices sounded choked.

Finally Jacob swung the whip, Louis slapped the neck of the Indian pony he was riding, and they were off to the green Willamette Valley.

On both banks of that hospitable river pioneers had established tiny villages. Portland, near the confluence of the two waterways, was a busy harbor for river boats and for merchantmen from Boston and the Sandwich Islands. Farther upstream were Oregon City, Salem, and Eugene.

Only three years ago, a New York settler had built a little place by the roadside. He named it Albany after the capital city of his home state. Now a small cluster of homesteads nestled in a bend of the river, with a grist mill and an inn.

There Louis and Jacob decided to unload their wagon.

It was a good country. Almost anything would grow in the moist climate. The winters were mild and the cattle could be left to graze outdoors throughout the year. There were fish and game in abundance.

Louis and Jacob staked out their claim on some black bottomland near the spot where the Calapooya River empties into the Willamette. The strange name, Calapooya, is that of an Indian tribe which once roamed the valley.

Impatiently the new arrivals set to work with firebrands and then with the ax. The smell of burning brush hung heavily over the newly cleared land. Soon the surviving oxen began to pull the plow. Seeds that had been carefully carried across the plains were dropped into the loamy soil.

"Next week we'll start the house," said Louis, "and as soon as the roof is raised, I'll write to Hannah and send her the ticket."

The structure went up, but instead of a home for a young couple it became a frontier trading post. The brothers wanted to farm, but the neighbors kept on urging them to use their skills as merchants. It was Drakesville all over again. Albany had to have a store. Most anybody could farm, the villagers pleaded, but nobody else knew how to ship goods from Portland, how to get animals and produce to the market, and how to handle orders and invoices without getting completely bogged down.

The "Fleischner Place," as it was soon known around the valley, was not hard to find. At all times the blanket-draped figures of Indians could be seen squatting near the front steps. First they came only to barter but then, surprised at seeing themselves

treated with kindness and understanding, they returned for advice and help when caught in the con-
fusing ways of the white man. Both brothers soon
learned to speak the tribal dialect.

The walls of the store were covered with clumsily
written notices about things people wanted to buy
or sell, from used butter churns to old almanacs.
The trading post was the meeting place of the vol-
untary fire department. There town officials and
school directors were elected. On Sundays the Con-
gregational Church held its services at the Fleischner Place until its own modest sanctuary was finished.

And when danger threatened from the outside, it
was again in the pioneer store where the men collected to fight it off.

2

The slippery board walks of Albany groaned under
the impact of many caulked boots. Heavy rains had
turned the street itself into an almost impassable
mire, but now, for the first time in many days, the
sun burst through the clouds revealing the white-
capped peaks of the Cascade Range to the east.

However, the men in their coarse homespun
clothes had little interest in the scenery. They were

sticking their heads together trying to digest the news that was posted on the door of the Fleischner Place: new Indian uprisings in the Rogue River Valley. The army regulars were hard-pressed, and an urgent call had gone out for volunteers.

Inside the store, a sweating officer, his stained tunic unbuttoned, sat at a table heaped with papers, waiting for the first citizen of Albany to step forward and join the militia. Several men stood around, but stayed clear of the table.

"Your people here have no nerve for Indian-fighting," grumbled the officer as he turned to Louis Fleischner. "If everyone were like them, the redskins would soon drive us out of the whole Northwest. A defeat on the Rogue may mean the end of all the settlements from the California line to Puget Sound."

"You're right, Captain. But can't you see why these men don't want to go? They've sacrificed so much to get started here and now, when their first crops are about to be harvested, they hesitate to leave again. Besides, who'll protect their own homes when they're away?" one of the settlers answered.

"If they don't help out now and teach those brown savages a lesson, it's like sending them an invitation to raid their houses, burn their crops, and steal their children. Staying home for protection won't help much if we allow the enemy to mass and to attack several tribes strong."

"I tell you what, Captain," Louis Fleischner said. "Somebody has to make a start. Once the ice is broken, the others will follow. Sign me up. Jacob can take care of the store while I'm gone. And I don't have a family to worry about me—at least, not yet."

The officer hesitated.

"Go ahead, sign him up," said Jacob, who had been standing with the other men. "It's always this way. If he sniffs adventure, there's no holding him back. Just see that you return with your scalp still in the right place, Louis. With so many men coming home from the California mines for the winter, I should be able to hire some help. They're spoiled, though, and it'll cost me a pretty penny for wages. But we'll get along."

With fingers more used to gripping a saber than a pen, the captain wrote furiously. He finished with a flourish and then handed the pen to the new recruit for his signature.

"All right, my boy," he said, beaming with relief. "You're now Private Louis Fleischner of the Oregon Volunteer Militia. We're leaving tomorrow at daybreak for the Rogue. Who's next, gentlemen?"

The ice had indeed been broken. About a dozen more settlers stepped forward to sign the papers. Then they rushed home to break the news to their families and to get their packs ready.

3

The Rogue River Indians had been on the warpath for some time. Isolated settlers, often living miles away from the nearest neighbor, were at their mercy. Only charred marks of death and destruction remained when the war parties swooped down unexpectedly on the homesteads.

This time Chief Hawk of the Siskiyus had called on all the tribes of the winding valley to assemble at his war camp for a big strike. He was determined to clear southern Oregon of the white invaders, once and for all.

The United States Army was aware of his plans, but so far the forces available had been too weak for an all-out attack. It was a war of small cruel skirmishes. Nobody stuck to the rules.

Finally a sufficiently large expedition gathered at Fort Vancouver. By boat, on horseback, and on foot they moved south. Governor Lane himself was in command.

Then, one evening, they were all camped near the hamlet of Medford: the regulars of the Fourth U. S. Infantry, several companies of volunteers, and a band of friendly Klikitats. Under a cluster of trees stood a solitary howitzer which had been dragged along all the way from the Columbia River fort. It was not a very formidable looking piece of artillery, but in previous campaigns it had been found that the Indians were deadly afraid of the "fire-on-wheels."

The men huddled close to the bonfires playing dice or telling stories of older encounters with the red man. It was cold and damp. There was tension in the air. Everybody knew that the decisive hour of the campaign was at hand.

Scouts had returned with reports that all the Rogue River tribes were now concentrated in one large encampment on the opposite slope of the valley, just below a giant bluff. Chief Hawk had assumed the over-all command. The glow of distant campfires could be seen through the trees. Knowing that the showdown was near, the Indians had not even felt it necessary to conceal their fires.

In the governor's tent the officers were gathered to hold council. Louis was among them. A handy man with a pen and quick with figures, he had been given a commission within a few days and was now one of the governor's personal aides.

There had been some skirmishing during the day. A stray shot had hit the governor's arm; he wore it in a bloodstained sling.

Colonel Kearney, the senior officer, was pleading for an all-out attack at dawn:

"We have them cornered where they can't get away. It might take a month of hunting through the forest to find another time like this. The how- itzer could shell their camp easily and spread terror among the whole band. Then the troops would move in and finish them off. The approaches from three sides are heavily wooded and give excellent protection. We have a number of seasoned veterans from the Cayuse War, and the volunteers are spoil- ing for a fight. And may I suggest that we don't take any prisoners this time. The news of our victory will spread from tribe to tribe and teach them all a good lesson."

Governor Lane, a kind man who dearly loved the Northwest, was undecided. Once more he studied the map before him and then he looked through the tent opening up to the cloudy sky. His new aide spoke up. It was not quite the proper military way for a green lieutenant of the militia to break into the deliberations of higher ranking officers, who were always so scornful of those "uniformed back- woods farmers." But if it was all right with the gov- ernor, they could not very well object.

"I'm afraid," said Louis Fleischner, "it won't do. We've had already too much of that: attacks, repris- als, counter-reprisals, and so on in endless succes- sion. The Indians feel that fighting is their only chance for survival. They will continue to resist the settlers. Our victories will only make them more

cunning and savage. We must assure them that they
are not doomed."

"What'd you want us to do? Hold hands with
them?" asked the colonel impatiently. The lieutenant chose to overlook the remark.

"Do they know out here about the treaties our
government has made with tribes in other territo-
ries? They too could be given reservation lands and
live there undisturbed. We must negotiate with the
Rogue Indians. If Governor Lane promises them a
fair settlement, I'm sure the Congress in Washington will uphold him."

"The bullet and the hangman's noose are the
only language the redskin understands," muttered
an unshaven major.

"Your soldiers go back behind the stockades of
the forts," pleaded Louis, "but we stay here in the
open country, a thin, exposed line of white settlers.
We must have permanent peace. Indian and settler
can live side by side, if each feels secure, if each
trusts the other."

The governor looked at his twisted arm sling. His
face showed the pain of the wound. Yet he said:

"I think the storekeeper is right. We must come to
terms with the Indians. The only other way is to ex-
terminate them completely, and we certainly did
not come to the West to engage in wholesale murder.
Fleischner, will you take along an interpreter and
go to the Rogue camp to arrange for a powwow?"

This was a dangerous mission. A white flag of truce could mean very little to warriors in full warpaint. All eyes were on the tall volunteer. A contemptuous sneer spread over the major's face. He was expecting a lame excuse, an attempt to get out of the job of walking straight into the hands of an enemy who was thirsting for blood. But Louis said:

"I will go, Governor. I think I know the Indian mind. I have talked with many of them who consider me their friend. In spite of all their war dances and shouts, I'm convinced they want peace as much as we do."

"I hope you will know how to handle yourself," said the governor. "If the painted bucks get ugly, we might not be in time to pull you out alive. God be with you, boy. We'll be waiting for you."

Before dawn the envoy and his Klikitat companion slipped out of the silent camp. The hours went by slowly. Staying close to their stacked rifles, the men talked in low whispers. The sentinels kept a sharp lookout, their ears tuned in the direction of the Indian encampment. From time to time they heard muffled noises. Or was it only their imagination? Now it sounded like distant shouting. And what was this? Could it have been a shot? It was hard to tell.

The sun had climbed to its midday height. Still there was no sign of the envoy. In his tent the governor looked nervously at his timepiece.

"How long do we wait, Governor?" It was Colonel Kearney who interrupted his thoughts. "We should have heard from Fleischner by now. I wonder what finished him: a bullet in his chest or a tomahawk in his skull?"

"You don't put much trust in the power of words, do you, Colonel?"

"You don't fight Indians with words. Do I have your permission to give the signal to the howitzer crew? We could rout the whole gang by nightfall. If they slip away this time, heaven only knows when we will catch up with them again. You are well aware how anxious the militiamen are to go home to their plowing."

"It doesn't look good," admitted the governor. "We will wait another hour. Then, if nothing develops, you may take over."

The minutes ticked away slowly. The colonel was already whispering orders to his messengers. The company commanders were gathering around the map for the final briefing. On the knoll which commanded the view of the valley the cannoneers were getting their fuses ready.

Suddenly there was a stir throughout the camp. Soldiers and militiamen came running from all directions. Flanked by sentinels, the two emissaries emerged from the dense forest into the clearing. Wearily they dragged themselves toward the governor's tent. Louis' face was pale with exhaustion and with the suspense of the past hours. Practically the whole force followed the little procession, shouting questions and cheering.

"We made it, Governor," Louis said as he came to attention. His salute would have been a disgrace on the parade ground, but now nobody cared. "We talked for four hours. Several times I felt all was lost. A group of hotheaded young warriors clamored for a fight. They wanted the chief to have us seized and tortured as a reprisal for some recent mistreatment by whites. Do you know how hard it is to keep a straight face when cold fear runs through your body like an icy stream? For a while I wouldn't have bet a nickel that my scalp could stay on my head."

He fingered his skull tenderly as if to assure himself that the skin was still all there.

"I continued to reason with the chief. Pointing in the direction of the howitzer, I described its destructive medicine. I told him that the great white chief in Washington had many more men and fires-on-wheels and that he could never win out in the end."

The lieutenant swayed slightly. The governor pointed at a bench. Louis almost upset it when he sat down.

"The gestures of the young warriors became more threatening. But the old chief knew better. He's a clever fox. After what seemed to me hours of silence he raised his arm. The decision had been made. In the morning he will counsel with you at Table

Rock. You are to come with ten companions, unarmed. He pledges his sacred word as chief that you will not be harmed."

"Unarmed, eh? The old rascal. He has several hundred Siskiyus, all of them wizards with bow and arrow and quite a few also with British rifles."

"What are you going to do, Governor?" asked the colonel grimly. "The cannoneers are still waiting."

"Keep double guards posted and tell the men to take it easy for the rest of the day. I'm going tomorrow. You, Fleischner, are coming with me. I may need you."

4

Two days later the contingent of Willamette Valley volunteers was on its way home. A treaty had been signed on Table Rock promising the Indians a spacious reservation at Klamath Lake, financial help, and government protection against other tribes that might want to prolong the warfare. It was not the end of all difficulties, but for the moment the danger had passed. The pioneer communities west of the Cascades could now breathe easier and lay plans for the next season, unafraid of sudden violent attacks.

The men sang and joked. They also talked at great length about a short ceremony they had witnessed on the last day of the encampment:

The troops were drawn up in formation. What

soldiers and militiamen lacked in regulation uniform parts they made up in loud, boastful spirit. Finally a roll of drums that echoed from the surrounding hills brought them to silent attention. The governor called up Lieutenant Fleischner and made him step in front of the assembled force. He said, "I hereby appoint you a colonel of the militia and put you in charge of the Willamette Valley Volunteers. This is a small reward for the splendid service you have rendered to the Oregon Territory and to the cause of better human relations. You had the courage to stand up for your convictions in the face of scorn and derision. This is harder than braving the enemy, but you have done that too."

From now on it would be the Albany storekeeper's task to recruit and train his neighbors in the art of warfare and to lead them should it again become necessary to defend their valley by arms.

From private to colonel in one campaign was quite a jump. But this was not the regular army. The homesteaders needed leaders badly and, when one was found, there was no time to have him work up gradually through the ranks.

Proud of their illustrious fellow citizen, the small band of Albany volunteers returned to their home base. Soon Louis was again entrenched behind the store counter. But now it was "Give me a pound of salt, Colonel," or, "Colonel, can you get me a new harness from Portland?"

🌲🌲🌲🌲🌲🌲 *The waiting is over*

Several homesteader families were returning from their annual shopping trip to Portland.

Slowly the little sternwheeler pushed upstream, leaving in its wake a trail of white foam. With caution it nosed around the many bends of the Willamette River. At times the banks were steep and high, then again they sloped gently down from the fields and pastures of the valley. Rows of slender birch waved greetings, their silvery leaves sparkling in the afternoon sun.

The deck was protected by gray awnings, and above them the tall black smokestack stretched skyward. The wooden planks shuddered under the rhythmic clanking of the gears in the belly of the boat. With a satisfied grin the captain surveyed the large crowd of passengers. Children played among the trunks and had the time of their lives climbing over crated goods of all kinds.

It had been a good year, and after the long toil of the summer they welcomed the enjoyment that a few days of city life offered. There were theaters and musicals, and the ladies were dressed in the latest fashions. The amusements of Portland were something to talk about till the next autumn came around.

From time to time the mournful sound of the whistle announced that the steamboat was getting ready for a stop. Teams and wagons waited at each landing. Passengers trooped across the shaky gangplank to shore, and new ones lugged their bundles onto the boat.

Looking around the deck to find acquaintances, their eyes alighted on a group in holiday dress gathered by the stern near the wheelhouse which hid the enormous splashing paddles. Hardly anybody failed to recognize one man in this company.

"How goes it, Colonel?" they usually called out. "Had a nice trip?"

Louis Fleischner acknowledged each greeting with a few friendly words and turned again to his travel companions.

"You seem to be known by everybody in this part of the country," said a young man with whiskers and sideburns. "What is the secret of your popularity, Mr. Fleischner?"

"There is nothing strange about it, Mr. Fried. It's just the fact that I've lived in this valley for nearly six years. Traveled about a good deal. When you're a trader among pioneers, a militia officer, a town councilman, fire chief, and what not, you can't help knowing everybody. But I love it."

"It's beginning to be the same way with me," said Moses Fried. "My little crossroads place in Dayton has already become a landmark. They call it Fried's Corner as if it had been there for ages."

Others in the little group spoke of similar experiences, among them Edward Cahn, Isaac Selling, and Isaac Jacobs of Oregon City and Goodman Bettman and Sam Friendly from Eugene. They were all young Jews and they talked in German or in a heavily accented English.

Every one of them had come to America within the last few years, and most had continued to the Northwest by way of Panama and California. They were now at home in various small towns and hamlets along the river.

It was easy to see that something thrilling had recently happened to them. Their talk never strayed far away from it. They came from a visit to the first Jewish community west of the Rocky Mountains and north of California. Congregation Beth Israel had been founded only a few months ago, just in time to prepare services for the High Holidays.

"You've got to admire these Portland men," said Edward Cahn. "They really have faith in the future of the Northwest. If they didn't believe that many more Jews would come to live and to raise children around here, they wouldn't have gone through the trouble of founding Beth Israel."

"I think they elected the right man to be the first president of the congregation," remarked Sam Friendly. "Leopold Mayer's full of enthusiasm. Talks already of a big synagogue building."

"Well, some day perhaps," said Isaac Jacobs. "Right now this is a little farfetched. You saw where the services were held: in a bare upstairs room."

"I had a hard time keeping my mind on the prayers," confided Cahn, "with all that noise coming from the blacksmith shop and the livery stable below. I wonder where Laski, the *chazzan*, studied singing, if you can call it singing. Most of the time it sounded more like wailing."

"And the Torah scroll and the *shofar*," added Jacobs, "had to be borrowed from San Francisco. Even so they almost didn't get to Portland in time. Mr. Mayer was already frantic when the boat finally arrived, a full day late."

"Granted," said Friendly. "It was not like Yom Kippur at the Great Synagogue in Prague nor even at the Wooster Street *shul* in New York. But just imagine: a *minyan* on the farthest corner of the world where, till a few years ago, only Indians and a few Canadian trappers roamed the woods. The old-timers down at Erickson's Saloon must've really been surprised when they heard us chant the *Kol Nidre*. Some even ran out into the street to see what was going on."

"Yes, Portland is coming along," remarked Isaac Selling. "I'm sure one day it'll be a large city."

"That may be so," countered Sam Friendly. "Yet I like it where I am. Eugene's only a tiny place, but to me it's home. People stop at my store whenever they pass by, whether they want to trade or not. And I've always time to listen to a neighbor."

"You're getting to be quite a big man up at Eugene, I hear," said Louis Fleischner. "I'm told they want to make you the next mayor."

"Oh, there's been some talk. But they might change their minds. Perhaps they can't stomach the idea of a Jewish mayor."

"Come now, Sam. You know very well that it's different out here. Just before leaving on this trip, I learned that Reuben Alexander had been elected mayor of Pendleton. And I know of several other Jewish city fathers."

"In Astoria, down by the coast, they have one," said Selling.

"Once," continued the colonel, "they laughed about the idea of Jews roughing it in this primitive country, and look what's happened. There's hardly

a farm village or mining town in the whole Northwest that has not at least one Jewish trader or
rancher, and he's usually head over heels mixed in
community affairs."

"Yes," added Sam Friendly, "come to think of it,
at the *minyan*, practically all the out-of-towners
were councilmen, postmasters, or schoolboard members. The man who blew the *shofar* sits in the Terri-
torial Legislature."

"If you talk about Jews in public life," interrupted Goodman Bettman, "don't forget our colonel here. Every white man seems to know the hero
of the Rogue War, not to speak of the Indians who
worship him."

"You're pouring it on rather thick, Goodman,"
said the colonel. "But it's truly amazing how our
people have taken their places in this new frontier
society. I feel the Jewish pioneer merchant belongs
right with the French-Canadian fur trader and the
Methodist circuit rider to the great romantic figures
of the Northwest."

"Have you heard about the little town in eastern
Oregon that was founded by Henry Heppner?"
asked Isaac Jacobs. "They're going to name it after
Henry. He was against it, but he was overruled.
Naming a town after a Jew—it couldn't have hap-
pened in Bohemia."

The steamer strained against the current. Slowly
it drifted by the fields and orchards. The trees were

heavy with red and yellow apples. Rabbits were playing among the stubble. Many passengers had disembarked at the various whistle stops. Of the little group at the stern only those bound for Albany and Eugene were still on board.

The children were asleep on the hard benches. Even the grownups felt drowsy from the endless thudding of the engine below.

Sam Friendly shook himself awake from a short nap and turned to Louis Fleischner:

"Say, Louis. I just remembered that your brother Jacob said goodbye to us, right at the end of the Yom Kippur service."

"Yes, he's going back east."

"There was such a confusion. We were all wishing each other a good year and then rushing off to prepare for the return trip. I was already on the boat when I remembered Jacob. Why's he leaving? Is he tired of the Northwest? Too much of a struggle?"

"On the contrary, Sam. He's bringing home a bride. When he went to high school in Tachau, he met a girl named Fannie Nadler. They exchanged secret little notes in school, and at the close of the Sabbath they walked hand in hand along the old town moat. It was the usual childhood romance. But out of it blossomed real love, a love that withstood separation for many years. They wrote each other occasionally. They had promised to wait for one another. And now it has happened."

"Is your brother planning to stay in the East with his bride?"

"Not at all. Right now he is riding again on the Oregon Trail, only this time in the opposite direction. It won't take him long because he's impatient and he's traveling light. Fannie 'll meet him in New York where they plan to get married. Their honeymoon will be the long return voyage by sea, first southward on the Atlantic Ocean, around Cape Horn, and then up along the coast of Mexico, California, and Oregon."

"Well, here's the start of another Jewish family."

"That's what all the boys 're doing. They come, carve out their place in the community, and then they go back to get a Jewish bride from the Old Country."

"I know it. Took the trip myself two years ago, and it was worth it: every mile of sandstorms, heat, and seasickness. When I came to my old Bavarian hometown, there was Jennie ready to follow me to the end of the world."

"Yes, she's a wonderful pioneer woman."

"Our baby's still too small for the Portland trip, so Mother had to stay home too. But come next Rosh Hashana, with God's will, they'll come along unless, of course, there'll be another one on the way. And what about you, Louis? Shouldn't the older brother have set a shining example?"

"I've been waiting for the question. I hear it,

sooner or later, wherever I go. It's so hopeless to explain all this. People probably think I'm a little crazy. Believe me, I want a home and a family just like the rest of you men. But there's that girl from Vogelsang. As soon as I'm face to face with another girl, my tongue freezes up. The thought of another woman taking Hannah's place in my heart gives me almost physical pain."

"And what about Hannah?"

"I've written her dozens of times from Oregon, but no answer. She may've forgotten me. After all, we were only children then. But, on the other hand, lots of things can happen to letters that are carried by express riders and then taken across the Atlantic and through half of Europe. She may be sick or even dead. But I've waited so long, I may as well wait for my brother's return. Surely Fannie 'll know something. Perhaps she's carrying a message for me."

His friend looked at him, deep concern showing in his eyes.

"Don't wait too long, Louis. We've only this one life to live. It is too short to be wasted on a dream. You know what lonely men look like when they get older. The mining camps and the waterfronts of our ports 're full of them."

"I know. It sounds all so foolish. But I've made up my mind to wait for Jake's return. It won't be too long."

2

Again the Fleischner Place was well filled with customers and with those who just wanted to pass the time of day. Once more the talk was about gold, and mining tools were in short supply.

The men stood around, rhythmically chewing their wads of tobacco, and, from time to time, aiming a volley at the big brass spittoon in the corner. Fortunately most were good marksmen.

Slim Parks shifted his load from one cheek to the other. At night he would have frightened the children with his long matted hair and unkempt beard. His frame was thin and bent, and he was untidy all the way from his mangy beaver cap to his muddy boots.

"This Orofino Mine in Idaho's really hot," he said. "Out in th' woods, while I's looking after my traplines, I met all kinds o' fellows talking 'bout th' Idaho gold fields. I tell you, it's a regular rush. Many 're getting ready to go."

"You think there'll be paydirt like in California?" asked a young farmer.

"No guarantee, of course. You know what happened to all the rumors about rich lodes in southern and eastern Oregon. This may be a dud too.

And yet, maybe it's the real thing. A fellow got to take his chance. I'll hop on the Portland boat as soon as she comes back from Eugene. And then off we go up the Columbia and on to Orofino. Want to be there before the news gets out an' the crowds come swarming from all over the country."

The young farmer turned to the proprietor of the store:

"I don't suppose you'd be interested in staking out a claim in Orofino, Colonel? I'm itching to go myself, but I've a wife and three young'uns at home. They need me. If I were in your shoes—"

"I know all about it, Andy. I'm single, free to go where I please. Heard it often enough. But it so happens that I like it here. Besides—"

The long whining sound of the boat whistle rose from the river and pierced the quiet of the town.

All morning Louis had kept glancing through the open door in the direction of the steamer landing. He had been visibly nervous and absentminded.

"The Portland boat," he shouted, pushing aside customers and idlers alike. "Jacob and his wife ought to be on the boat and perhaps— So long, men. You'll excuse me. The store's closed for the remainder of the day."

He was gone before the surprised bystanders knew what was happening. They shook their heads in wonderment, collected their purchases, and dispersed slowly up and down the street.

3

Two hours later the ocean travelers were seated with Louis in the freshly painted upstairs parlor room. The whole second story of the frame building had been remodeled in honor of the bridal pair.

Refreshments were spread on the table. Trunks, some hastily opened, but not yet unpacked, wraps and pieces of clothing littered the room. Jacob had grown a shiny black mustache which he kept carefully oiled and twirled so it would point upward. He was dressed in a modish suit and he wore a stiff high collar. A long golden watch chain dangled from his checkered vest.

He was talking continuously and with gusto. His roving eyes returned again and again to the small oval face of his wife, a slender, dark-haired beauty whose soft brown eyes were now heavy with the fatigue of long, strenuous travel.

Jacob was in the midst of a glowing report on their marvelous trip. With relish he described the elegance found in the cities of the east coast. He talked of the brown-skinned islanders in the Caribbean Sea, the bleak, wind-swept shores of Patagonia. He described the foods of Chile and the dances of the Mexicans. He brought news and greetings from many friends who had settled in California.

Louis made brave attempts to listen, but his mind was plainly on another matter. Finally he could contain himself no longer. His brother was just giving an elaborate description of an opera performance in San Francisco when he broke in:

"What about Hannah?"

The newlyweds looked at each other in embarrassment. They had known that this moment would come, sooner or later. Often they had talked about it and dreaded it. Now it was here.

"Fannie knew Hannah well," began Jacob. "They had been schoolmates in Tachau. Everybody called Hannah the most beautiful girl in town. In the first years after you'd left she often spoke of you and of America. She wanted to know all about life in the West, about keeping a Jewish home out here. Proudly she showed your letters to everybody. Then a change came over her. She never mentioned the name of her childhood playmate any more. Hastily she changed the subject when it came up. She wanted to forget. She had waited too long for an event that failed to happen. At least, it didn't happen in time. Her mother, a widow, was desperately poor. When the matchmaker, the *shadhan,* came to the house, he told them of a wealthy jeweler, a widower himself, who wanted Hannah for a wife. Now she lives in Prague and has several children. Whether your letters of recent years were ever forwarded to her, we don't know."

For a long time Louis sat stunned. When he finally spoke, it was with a halting, uneasy voice:

"I see. Nobody can blame her. I should have acted sooner. Well, the curtain's down. The play is over."

He got up and went to the door while the couple remained seated, not knowing what to do next.

"Make yourselves at home. The whole upstairs is yours. I've moved my things to the little room behind the store. Now, if you'll excuse me, I'm going out to see a customer."

Without any aim he sauntered along the boardwalk, not recognizing anybody. Astonished heads turned after him. This was not at all like the colonel who always had a smile for everybody.

At the street corner the ears of the lonely stroller were assailed by the noise of many rough voices coming from the town saloon. With unsteady steps a disheveled man stumbled outside.

The colonel hailed him:

"Hey, Slim, when 're you leaving for Orofino?"

"Oro-, Oro-f-fino," the drunkard stammered. "Nothin' doin'. Just lost all my money in a poker game. Gave th' bartender my mining gear to pay for th' whiskey. A guy got to drown his loss. Not a red cent left. So I'm not goin' anywhere."

"Oh, yes, you are. I'll stake you to grub and to some new gear, and I'm going with you. Better be sober when the boat comes back from Eugene. We'll both be off for Idaho and the gold."

🌲🌲🌲🌲🌲 *Full steam into the wilderness*

The roar of the Celilo Falls nearly drowned out the rumbling of carts, the clatter of hoofs, and the shouts of voices. The portage road which led around the falls was only a crude trail, just a pair of parallel ruts dug by wagon wheels.

Louis Fleischner and Slim Parks were in the lead of the group. Their backs were bent low under the burden of heavy packs. Others led sluggish mules. A few two-wheeled ox-drawn carts followed. The men had been passengers on a Columbia River boat which had carried them up to the falls. From there they had to take to their feet.

The procession now emerged from the forest that lined the river and made its way to a stretch of open gravel beach. Louis looked back to the rapids, fascinated by the spectacle.

The salmon were jumping over the falls. Without letup, they hurled their silvery bodies against smooth boulders working themselves upstream inch by inch. With giant leaps they shot into the air to reach the next step on their tiring journey. If they were lucky enough to fall into a shallow indentation filled with water, they rested a while before dashing themselves again into the foaming rapids. Many, less fortunate, landed high and dry. For them it was the end of the mysterious journey. But the others pushed on, working themselves closer and closer to their spawning grounds high up in the mountains.

Every year the salmon came inland from their ocean playgrounds, driven by an unknown force, seeking a place they had left many, many months ago, when they were newly born fingerlings. An unerring instinct led them back exactly to the same spot in the rugged highlands where they had been born.

Louis observed that the valiant jumpers had other dangers to contend with beside the steep rocks that jutted from the river bed. Balancing on the edges of the crags were the lean figures of Indians, spears in hand. As far back as their legends could tell, the people of the tribe had gathered on this spot during the season of the salmon run. By the time the fish had come this far, they were tired and slow. Then the spears would descend with lightning speed.

Suspended between trees on the bank were the lines of rope from which the salmon, cut into strips, were hung to dry. This was strengthening food which would keep the Celilo Indians alive for the remainder of the year.

After a few moments of rest, Louis shifted his burden and continued toward the edge of the river. There heavy pilings had been driven into the bottom and boards nailed over them to form a crude landing dock. A small steamer lay tied up, gently rocking as the current lapped against its stern. The name, *Colonel Wright,* was painted in large black letters on the white hull.

On the bridge stood the bearded skipper, a powerfully built man clad in shapeless, soiled oilskins. Pushing back his faded blue vizor cap, he shouted to the pilot who stood by the railing near the gangway:

"Look, Baughman, what's coming up the portage road!"

"They must've sent up another ship from Portland," said the stringy little man who was supposed to know every inch of the channel between Astoria and the Big Bend. "The company's probably stripped all the other river runs of ships so they can haul more miners to Idaho. There's money in this boom."

"Yes, men bound for the gold fields don't haggle over the fare. Can we take on any more?"

"She's getting mighty crowded, Captain White. We can squeeze some in, I suppose, but that won't give them much privacy."

"Who cares about privacy? This is not an ocean-going ship. They'll take this, or they can walk all the way to Orofino."

"Sure, Captain, if you say so. But don't forget, we need more space for fuel. Got to load cordwood for the engine. Trees'll be scarce from here on till we reach the Idaho forests."

Lem White, the skipper, leaned forward till he almost lost his balance. Cupping his hands over his mouth, he bellowed with a voice that matched the roar of the rapids:

"Hurry up, boys. Give 'em the ax. Time to cast off. No use waiting 'round with a full cargo."

This outburst of vocal thunder was addressed at three men on shore. Looking up from their back-breaking task, they wiped the sweat from their foreheads and lowered the double-bladed axes for a moment. Then they continued to cut a deep swath into the dense forest.

Now most of the prospectors had reached the dock. They unloaded carts and pack animals and carried their gear to the gangway. Captain White looked down on his prospective passengers, a mixed lot that only the lure of gold could bring together. All ages were represented from grizzled veterans to pink-cheeked youngsters still awaiting their first growth of beard. Some had the white hands of city dwellers, but most were rugged, sunburned outdoor characters, dressed in buckskin or heavy wool. They were unshaven and clearly in need of bathing. There was no woman in the group.

Louis looked up to the captain's bridge. The checkered shirt flapped loosely about his thin frame. He had lost weight since leaving Albany. But his eyes sparkled. Adventure awaited him. There was no time now for personal grief.

"Hey, Captain," he shouted, "can you take us on?"

"Where you bound?" asked the skipper's foghorn voice.

"Orofino. The mines."

"I thought so. Come aboard. We'll make room for you somehow."

"How far 're you going?"

"What a question. Orofino, of course. Isn't this where you're headed?"

"Surely. But you're not taking the boat all the way up the Clearwater River to Orofino. That's impossible."

"Nothing's impossible for my ship. Where there's water, the *Colonel Wright* goes. She was built for the rapids and the eddies."

"But no steamboat has gone farther up than the mouth of the Snake. This is not an Indian canoe."

"No, but it's the best darn sternwheeler in

the Northwest. Built for taking punishment. We stripped 'er down to make room for the most powerful engine in the business."

"So you plan to make it all the way to the gold fields?"

"That's what I said, young man. We steam up the Columbia and into the Snake, then up the Snake into the Clearwater, and up the Clearwater straight to Canal Gulch. There you can jump over the side and start panning right away."

"And here I was hoping to catch a boat ride for a hundred miles or so, at best, to shorten the long hike through the woods."

"Well, fellow, I can't make small talk with you all day. We're in a hurry. The *Colonel Wright* is casting off as soon as the cordwood is loaded. There'll be more miners waiting for us at the portage when we come back. So make up your mind!"

"I'm coming, skipper. Whether you make it as far as Orofino or not, this promises to be fun. I wouldn't want to miss it."

In spite of the captain's gruff threats, it took several hours till the *Colonel Wright*'s huge paddlewheel started to splash. The pilot turned her bow against the current, and soon the land began to flatten out into long waves of brownish hills. Slowly the towering Cascade Range receded into the distance. For a time, snow-capped Mount Hood still peaked above the timberline till, after another bend in the river, it too disappeared.

Skillfully Baughman steered the heavily loaded vessel around and in between the many grotesquely shaped islands, some so large that deer and pheasant fed on them comfortably, others just needles of dark rock piercing the water surface. The frail man who looked like a tramp on land was now the master of many destinies. With an unerring eye he found the unmarked channel, never showing the slightest doubt which way to turn in this maze of coves and inlets.

The lower deck which was politely called the cabin was a clutter of bundles, trunks, and heaps of tools. Men sat on whatever they could find or they lay stretched out snoring loudly, their greasy felt hats covering their faces. At each end of the oblong room a dice game was in progress. Above the shouting and swearing of the players could be heard the clang of the little cubes as they rolled over the bottoms of two upturned barrels.

It was late in the afternoon, and Louis felt lonely despite the crowd around him. The smoke of many pipes and the strong odor of unwashed bodies made the air thick and heavy. Slim, Louis' travel companion, was deeply engaged in shooting the dice. He was likely to keep going till he ended up flat broke.

Louis wanted to breathe clean, fresh air. Quietly

he slipped out of the cabin and climbed the narrow
ladder to the upper deck which was nothing but
the roof over the cabin. It commanded a wide view;
only the captain's bridge protruded above it. The
ship was just entering the Big Bend, a sweeping
arch indicating the river's change of course from
north-south to a westerly direction.

The former storekeeper inhaled the moist breeze
eagerly. The small flocks of white cumulus clouds
were beginning to turn rosy. A deep peace rested
over the silent, sharply cut valley. For the first time
since he had fled from his defeat, Louis almost felt
at ease.

As his eyes swept around to take in the wide panorama, he saw a solitary figure. A man was standing at
the bow facing upstream. Louis was surprised that
there were other passengers who wanted to enjoy
the quiet beauty of a river sunset.

He felt drawn to the stranger and he began to
walk over toward the bow. The man seemed to be a
little younger than Louis, not much over twenty. He
was slender, but not very tall. Dark hair showed underneath his hat, and his clothes were well cut without appearing to be dandyish.

Louis was now directly behind the young traveler
who had not moved from his position. He was about
to step beside him and make some casual remark
about the scenery. But suddenly he stopped to take
another look. The young man was slightly sway-

ing, backward and forward, and, hardly audible, a steady stream of words formed into a peculiar melody came from his lips.

For a while Louis was too startled to decide upon his next step. This was— No, it could not be. Not here of all places, on a steamboat full of half-drunk miners. Yet, there was no mistake. Louis knew these movements and these sounds. They could only mean one thing: a Jew saying his evening prayers in the traditional way.

Noiselessly he fell a bit behind and waited. The other man was too deeply engrossed in his devotions to notice anything. With eyes closed he pronounced the *Sh'ma* and continued with the psalms and the benedictions that comprise the *Ma'ariv* ritual. It came over his lips so fluently, without any apparent effort, that it must have been ingrained in his memory through the habits of many years.

Just as he took three small steps backward to say the last "Amen," Louis called, *"Sholem aleichem."* Now it was the young worshipper's turn to be startled. At the sound of the ancient Hebrew greeting he whirled around. For a moment he just gasped, unable to speak.

Louis laughed. "Sorry to have frightened you, but I couldn't resist the temptation. I'm Louis Fleischner, lately from Albany in the Willamette Valley, now bound for Orofino, and extremely pleased to meet another Jew on this journey."

"This is indeed a wonderful surprise. I've heard of you, but I thought you were still training the militia and dabbling in politics. It is good to find you here so unexpectedly. I'm Julius Loewenberg from Portland."

"I suppose you're itching to get your hands on some heavy bags of gold, like the others."

"Panning will only be a spare-time occupation for me. I'm going to Idaho as a packer. My partner Leopold Seidner and I run a general merchandising business, but lately there wasn't enough going on to keep both of us busy. When the news of the gold rush spread, I thought that all the miners will need supplies. So I brought with me a cargo of beans, tobacco, flour, and some odds and ends."

"How'll you get all this through the woods of Idaho? There are no roads and no settlements."

"I don't know yet how I'll reach the camps, but somehow I hope to make it. I'm not only thinking of the profit. Those men must have goods or they'll starve and freeze to death. Already I've heard stories that scurvy had broken out at Orofino."

"I'm sure you'll be welcome wherever you turn up. If the captain knows what he's doing, you won't have to drag your wares too far. But I've my doubts."

"We'll see. I'll travel on the *Colonel Wright* as far as she goes. Then I'll have to rely on mules and burros. I've hiked through the wilderness before.

When I first decided to head westward from St. Louis, I took passage to Panama and then I packed across the Isthmus driving a herd of cattle before me. Believe me, it was hot. Never in my life was I so glad to see water than on that day when we reached the Pacific Ocean."

The two men found much to talk about and during the long days on the boat they became good friends. Julius greatly admired the more experienced pioneer, and Louis found in his new companion a kindred soul, eager like himself to strike out into untamed regions. For hours they stood on deck and talked about their religion, their former homes, and the reasons that had taken them so far away.

Julius had grown up in a small Prussian town. He too was unwilling to be satisfied with the narrow, humiliating life of the Jewish resident. And so he came to this country where he could spread his wings and be free in the company of free men.

2

The ship had entered the Snake River and was churning along in the brownish water. Above the dark rock walls of the canyon spread the meadow. In broad sweeps the carpet of wildflowers covered the hills and rolled down, here and there, to the edge of the river. For days no sign of human life could be detected.

Then, one morning, the *Captain Wright* nosed around a projecting cliff. "Look here," shouted Louis to his friend. "A whole village of Indians."

"They're so close," said Julius, "you can hear the babies crying. By the way, where are the men? I see only women and children."

"Probably out hunting. They sometimes stay away for many days."

The women looked up from their work as they heard the puffing of the steamer and then, shrieking with terror, they took off to the hills dragging their naked children behind them. The smoke-belching monster on the river, the like of which they had never seen, was too much even for a race trained to control their emotions. Within seconds the village was completely deserted. Only a few hungry dogs were still scratching among the dying cooking fires.

From then on the river travelers had constant company though it remained mostly unseen. The message of the fire-spouting apparition was carried before them by sleek canoes, by swift runners, and by the beat of the drums. The alarm was out in the whole valley.

As the passengers leaned idly over the railing, they could occasionally catch a glimpse of motion-less bronzed figures outlined against the sky. When the clanking ship drew nearer, the figures disappeared behind some outcroppings of rock, only to be waiting again farther upstream. Obviously the curious natives were hurrying to the scene from far and wide to get a good look at the "fire boat," as they had named it. They were fascinated, but they preferred to watch from a safe distance.

Captain White was not overly disturbed. He was in Nez Percé country, and this magnificent tribe had always been friendly to the white man. The skipper was eager to trade with the Indians. The cook's supplies of meat and fresh produce were running low, and in Julius Loewenberg's crates were lots of the shining trinkets the Nez Percés liked so well. But, as yet, they were too timid to come close.

In the meantime, passengers and crew settled down to a comparatively easy life. Louis was glad that the paying guests were expected to share some of the work with the hired hands. It gave him a chance to exercise arms and legs. Once a day they went on land in search of wood. Often they had to range pretty far inland before they could get a good-sized load.

Usually there was still considerable time left till the skipper would give the sign to move on. Then Louis got his trusted rifle and set out, with Julius, to hunt for game. Pheasants were plentiful, and Julius was thrilled to learn from the practiced woodsman the art of marksmanship.

On board much of the table talk was carried on at the expense of Brad, the cook. But he seemed to take pride in all the good-natured abuse that was heaped upon his bulky frame three times a day. He enjoyed the popularity, and his little eyes twinkled above the fat cheeks as he heard himself called every known synonym for rascal and nincompoop. When the men grew tired of talking about food, they fell back on their eternal topic: gold. Hot tips were passed on, plans were designed how to acquire great fortunes in a hurry and how to spend them most pleasantly afterward.

"Canal Gulch's the place," said one miner. "That's where I'm going to start panning. Why, a man can easily make eighty dollars a day or more, just placer mining, if he has any kind of luck at all."

"You can stay at Canal Gulch," said another. "But I'm moving higher up to Smith's Gulch. I've a hunch, the higher you climb the better the vein you find."

So they argued endlessly, throwing around colorful names like Baboon Gulch, Buffalo Hump and Elk City, names that were now famous, though only a few weeks ago they meant nothing at all.

"Have you picked your gulch already, Louis?" asked Julius. "Or do you plan to try them all out?"

"It's strange. The closer we come to all this hidden riches, the less interested I become. What does it really matter in the end how many bags of dust you carry away with you?"

"Fine attitude for a gold miner, I must say."

"Perhaps I'm more a tramp than a miner. I just want to go where the going is tough."

"If this is all you want, why don't you come in with me as a packer? It would be grand to have you for a partner, and I can assure you the going will be tough enough for you."

"The proposition sounds inviting. We'll talk about it some more."

Finally the *Colonel Wright* arrived at the junction of the Snake with its tributary. A high mountain towered to the left, its flank plunging almost straight into the river. With full steam the vessel moved into the narrower, but swifter Clearwater.

All hands were still at breakfast when pilot Baughman called out from the bridge, "Look here, a whole army."

The narrow plain on the south bank was filled with a solid mass of Indians. They stood in long rows or sat on their ponies in full war regalia, motionless, silently staring at the advancing ship. Many had rifles cradled in their arms. The slopes above were crisscrossed with lines of more warriors moving down to the meeting place.

"Now what're we going to do?" asked Baughman.

"Seems the whole Nez Percé tribe's having a get-together here. They must've traveled for days. Shall we move on, Cap?"

"No, Baughman, we have to stop. Our wood bins are empty. Going upstream those danged engines eat up the wood as if it were spaghetti. Besides, you don't run away from Indians if you want to keep their respect. Look at this group in the center. What d'you think?"

"The tall fellow with the giant feather bonnet must be the top man. What a magnificent roan he rides. And those warriors crowding around him seem to be a picked bodyguard."

"Let's blow the whistle and see what happens."

Ranks broke in wild commotion at the shrill sound of the boat whistle. The seething mass of brown bodies stampeded up the slope. Only the leader and the athletically built guards around him stood firm facing the oncoming fire boat.

"What d'you know," said Julius who was standing with his new partner at their accustomed place right by the bridge. "The fellow has courage."

Louis took a closer look. "Captain, it's Chief Lawyer himself, the head of all the Nez Percés. No one else could command such a following. That can only mean that he wants to meet us."

In his usual ear-splitting command voice, the skipper shouted, "Stop the engine! Drop anchor!"

"But Cap," remonstrated the pilot, "this is risky

business. They outnumber us at least twenty to one."

"They're a friendly tribe."

"Yes, but there's no telling how they feel about our boat. They might think it's bad medicine and must be destroyed."

"I hope you don't mind my butting in," called Louis from below, "but I know the tribe pretty well. I advise you to take the chance. Chief Lawyer is a powerful man. His word means much up and down the Snake and its tributaries. You need to have him on your side if you want to operate in these waters."

"They're scared stiff of our engines," wailed the pilot. "As soon as we stop them we lose our advantage."

"I don't like for passengers to stick their noses into my business," grumbled the skipper. "But this time the shopkeeper's right. The Chief is known as an honorable man," and filling his chest with air he bellowed, "Drop the anchor!"

The crew was getting ready to lower the dinghy and row the captain ashore when a small flotilla of canoes pushed off the south bank and made straight for the silenced steamer. Half-naked braves were paddling rhythmically, keeping time with the help of a monotonous singsong. In the bow of the brightly painted lead canoe stood Chief Lawyer, erect and dignified.

Captain and pilot exchanged surprised glances. The Chief had decided to visit the ship. This took more than ordinary courage, for the average Indian's mind was constantly filled with hundreds of fears. For him the whole universe was populated by spirits always ready to harm the poor human who did not know how to humor them properly.

Indians had never before been allowed on board ship. Their visits could spell trouble. Like children they were apt to pick up anything that struck their fancy and, not quite understanding the idea of personal property, they could become very angry when reprimanded.

But this time there was no choice. Hundreds of armed Nez Percés were intently watching the proceedings from shore. So why not give the Chief the full charm treatment?

Quickly the skipper ducked below deck and slipped into his well-wrinkled dark blue dress uniform. Looking as pompous as an admiral of the fleet, he helped the giant Indian personally on deck. From his stock of goods Julius had hastily dug out a broad-brimmed black hat, several long-handled axes, and some pipes with painted meerschaum bowls. A low grunt indicated the Chief's satisfaction with the presents.

Then the captain took him on a tour of the ship. They poked into the engine room. They clambered over cans of oil and coils of rope. Finally they ended up at the galley where the cook had a kettle of boiled beef and beans ready. Shaved for the first time on this journey and wearing a fairly clean white cap, Brad ceremoniously handed the steaming bowls to the Chief and to his two companions who had followed him everywhere like shadows. The likeness of their features made it obvious that they were his sons. The little group ate standing up. Not a single muscle flicked in their impassive faces. Finally they shook hands with the captain after the white man's fashion and departed.

As the canoes were beached, the whistle sounded again. But this time, instead of running in fear, the whole mass of Indians broke into a tremendous cheer that echoed from the hills. They had their Chief back, safe and sound, after his unbelievable show of bravery.

On board ship too, everybody breathed easier. The white adventurers had passed an important test. Henceforth, as they moved into unknown territory where there were no protective forts, they could at least count on the help of the scattered tribesmen who roamed the plateaus in search of the camass root.

"Full steam ahead," roared the skipper, and the craft moved up the Clearwater, the gurgling mountain river that had never before carried anything larger than a canoe.

3

Soon the grassy slopes disappeared and a dark world of virgin timber enveloped them. The pine forest stretched steeply upward on both sides, shutting out all view except a narrow strip of sky. Sometimes the valley widened enough to afford a glimpse of the snow-capped Rocky Mountains in the distance.

The ship shook as it churned through the rapids. The whole framework of heavy timber shuddered as if it would fall to pieces at any moment. The hour of trial was here. Would the vessel live up to the boasts of her master?

With anxious eyes the prospectors lined the railing. Every time another stretch of the white-foaming rapid was conquered, they let out a wild cheer like spectators at a fist fight. Only there was more at stake on the Clearwater, and they knew it.

The boat was approaching a giant eddy. The onlookers saw sizeable logs caught in the whirlpool and turning crazily 'round and 'round. The banter and laughter had stopped. Even the passengers who had made a nuisance of themselves by giving unwanted advice to the pilot were now silent. The whole company held its breath.

The captain, who had been on the bridge for over

eight hours, watched the sternwheel spin. It could not move the ship a single inch. The onrushing water threw the hull around like a nutshell. When it scraped against the shallow bottom. it made a sickening sound.

The faces on the railing were greenish. "Turn 'er 'round," shouted one miner, "or we'll all be dashed to pieces."

"Not yet, brother," roared the skipper. "We're not giving up so easily. Now we'll see of what stuff she's made. All hands stand by, crew and passengers! I'm going to line 'er over the eddy."

A huge coil of extra-heavy rope was rolled to the bow. One end was tied to the capstan.

"Volunteers forward," shouted Lem White. "I need two men to go overboard and anchor the line to that big pine tree over there."

A moment of embarrassed silence followed. Everybody was intently examining some spot on the floor. The captain was getting ready for a stronger appeal when Louis shot a questioning glance at Julius. The young packer nodded slightly.

"All right, Captain," called the colonel. "Help us overboard. We'll go."

Strong hands supported them as they eased themselves into the water. Numbed by the ice-cold bath, they clambered upon the nearest boulder. From there they hopped to the next, using hands and feet to find holds on the slippery, cold surfaces. Finally they reached the solid bank. Dragging the heavy rope behind them, they struggled through the tangle of thistles and wild blackberry vines till they reached the forest giant that stood all by itself on a little knoll. They secured the rope and then fought their way back, using the line to guide them. Wet to the skin and thoroughly chilled, they climbed back on board.

Now all hands lined up. They formed a double row, leaving the rope between them. With both hands they grasped it and, at the command of the captain, they gave a mighty heave. The boat inched forward while the motion of the eddy caused it to weave sideways. Another pull and yet another. The center of the whirl had been reached.

"Heave ho!" thundered the captain. "Pull, men, pull! Don't slacken now! Let's do it again! Heave ho—"

Muscles bulged into tight knots on tattooed arms. Hands burned as the rope slid from under them.

Then there was a loud crash. In confusion the whole crowd tumbled to the deck. The line had broken.

Helplessly the boat drifted backward. The wild current carried it with terrifying speed against a sheer rock wall. Everybody expected the end. Loud curses mingled with awkward prayers.

The ship had its broadside turned against the current. But at the next moment, a whim of the enraged mountain stream swung it around so that the bow faced upstream once more.

Captain White had been in tight spots before. With the presence of mind that only an old river boatman can possess, he grasped his chance.

"Full steam back!" boomed his voice above the cracking and splintering. Mechanically the dazed crew obeyed. The craft backed downstream till quieter waters were reached.

Louis Fleischner groped in his memory for the words of a Hebrew benediction he had learned in *heder* many, many years ago. He was to say it when saved from the immediate danger of death. He could not recall the words. "Thank you, O God," he murmured instead. "Grant me the power to do something worthwhile with the life you have given me again today."

Lem White was a daring man, but he was no fool. This was too much, even for the *Colonel Wright*. He turned around and on the next day the boat tied up at the same spot where Chief Lawyer had waited for them. This was the end of the river journey.

The triangular space between the two merging rivers was ideal for a port. It already had a name, though not a single structure had been built there yet. A member of the first prospecting party to strike out for Orofino had called it Lewiston in honor of Meriwether Lewis, partner of William Clark. The two famous explorers had stopped here on their historical journey, almost sixty years earlier.

When Louis helped his friend unload the merchandise, he said:

"I think I learned a lesson yesterday. When you come so close to facing your Maker, you wonder about the purpose of life. I don't have the full answer yet, but I know that just running after danger isn't much of a purpose. Don't you think so too, Julius?"

✣✣✣✣✣✣ *Lure of the gold*

Lewiston had become a noisy boom town. Since lumber was scarce, the houses were nothing more than canvas tents boarded up on the sides. Day and night, crowds jostled in and out of the half dozen saloons which had flimsy muslin curtains stretched between wooden frames instead of walls.

Two years had passed since the *Colonel Wright's* first landing. Now a whole fleet of riverboats was plying between the rapids of the Columbia River and this gateway to the Idaho gold fields.

Louis Fleischner and Julius Leowenberg were down at the waterfront in one of the crude sheds that sheltered the goods waiting to be packed to the mines. Crates and barrels were scattered on the floor just as the stevedores had brought them from the ship the day before. Julius held a sheet of in-

ventory lists and was poking around the confusion
to see what was what.

The young merchant bent low to inspect how
much damage the staples had suffered from the
river journey. After a while he straightened his
cramped back with a satisfied look on his face.

"The stuff seems to be all right this time. In Portland they're finally beginning to learn how to wrap
the merchandise."

"No wonder," replied Louis, who was looking out
over the river. "You gave them very detailed instructions. Now they know better how much punishment the goods have to take on such a trip."

Julius stepped over some heaps of ironware and
stood beside his friend. For a while they were both
silent. Then the younger man said: "You know,
Louis. I'm not sure whether I've said this before or
not. But just in case there's any doubt, let me tell
you again how happy I am that you've come in with
me as a partner. I don't think I could've done it
without you."

Louis laughed. There was some sadness in his
laughter.

"Whatever I set out to do, I always end up selling
things, as my father and probably all my ancestors
did before me. Why can't we Jews ever get away
from this occupation?"

"You talk as if there were something dishonest
about being a merchant. Everybody knows that in

pioneer country the packer's job is at least as dangerous as the prospector's. In the evening the miner returns to his cabin, crude as it may be, while the packer struggles through the forest all night. Wolves don't attack mining towns, but they feel different about pack trains."

"Yes, getting fifty or sixty mules up to Canal Gulch is no picnic."

"And you've seen the faces of the men light up when they see us come. Our arrival means that they'll eat square meals again, at least for a while. They need people like you."

"That's what I always hear. They need me. They need somebody to sell 'em things, as if selling were all I was ever meant to do."

"You're doing a lot more than selling. For those men out there you're the carrier of news, the letter writer, lawyer, and general advisor. They may be a rough lot, loud and uncouth, but underneath the surface they're just children who need their mother. You've the talent of making them comfortable. You're—"

He interrupted himself and jumped for the door. "Now what in blazes is this? Not another holdup?"

In a split second Louis was beside him.

"Sounds like Henry Plummer's on the job again. I wonder how long the people will stand for it."

Three loud reports had halted the friendly argument. The shots came from the Blue Ox Saloon down the block. In their wake arose a single outcry, a long wail so full of pain that it chilled the blood of the listeners. A babble of excited voices followed, and then there was silence.

A few moments later the muslin curtains of the makeshift drinking place parted, and slowly a man strode out. He was dressed in brand new gaudy clothes with all the creases still in place. A sombrero of soft light gray felt shaded his dark eyes that had an evil, contemptuous look. With studied careless-ness he shoved a pistol back into his coat pocket.

He sauntered down the street whistling through his teeth, trying hard not to appear in a hurry. The two packers now stood in the doorway of their shed. As he reached them the outlaw stopped and looked them over from head to toe. The long scar on his smoothly shaven right cheek was a dull red. It turned his haughty grin into a frightening grimace.

"Ah, our Jewish gentlemen." He pretended he had only now recognized them. "I hope you didn't mind the little commotion we just had at the Blue Ox. Only a small misunderstanding that I had to correct. Hope everybody got the point. As for you two, I've wanted to have a chat with you for some time."

"I don't know of anything we have to talk about," said Louis coldly.

"Just a little proposition I've in mind."

"We know your propositions, Plummer. One day you'll overreach yourself, and that'll be your end."

"I appreciate your concern, but don't you worry about me. Everybody here is scared stiff of me because people have found out that my predictions always come true. This reputation is the basis of my success."

"The shooting at the Blue Ox, was that also one of your predictions?"

"Certainly. Now as to my proposition. I have advised you before to retain my—er—personnel for your protection, at a slight fee, of course. You know, the pack trails are long and lonely. Wild animals and wild men lurk around, especially on your way back to Lewiston when you carry hundreds of dollars worth of gold dust."

"We understand you perfectly. But we'll just trust our luck and our rifles."

"Suit yourselves, gentlemen. Some people won't be reasonable. Too bad. It always hurts me deeply when I hear about fatal accidents in the woods."

Swaggering, he disappeared around the corner.

As soon as he was out of sight, the crowd spilled from the saloon into the street. Four men carried a silent, blanket-draped figure in the direction of the undertaker's house. The others remained standing in front of the entrance. Louis and Julius walked over to join them.

"It's a deadly shame," cried a short, stout man, his face purple with the indignation he had held back so long. "Here we are, a whole town full of men, and all of us at the mercy of the Plummer gang. In broad daylight he walks into the saloon and shoots down a man just because he had suggested that we form a vigilante committee."

"We've got to do something fast," said the bespectacled editor of the town weekly, "or nobody in the Idaho Territory 'll be safe. The gang is getting bolder every day."

Louis whispered, "Look how everybody's bursting with courage as soon as Plummer turns his back. At the Blue Ox, a little while ago, nobody had anything to say."

"Can you blame 'em?" asked Julius.

"I suppose not. Their own skins are closest to their bones," and turning to the whole crowd, Louis raised his voice:

"We're paying the price of being successful. Where there's wealth, the parasites show up. As long as the arm of the American government cannot reach this far, we must band together for our protection."

"But how do we go about it?" asked the possessor of the big round stomach. "Plummer's quicker on the draw than anybody else around here."

"He can't shoot down a whole platoon of determined citizens. If you want a peaceful town, you must follow the advice for which that man lost his life. You must have law and law enforcement. I am willing to join the vigilantes. Who else?"

For a moment the crowd was taken aback by the direct approach. A few shot furtive glances around, perhaps to see if Plummer was not lurking somewhere in the background. The town scribe jerked his head nervously so that the spectacles slipped off his long nose. Forgotten, they dangled from a black silken cord as he asked:

"Who's going to be the commander? We need somebody who can face up to Henry Plummer. Otherwise he'll just pick us off one by one. I'll join if we have the right leader."

Julius cast a long glance at his friend. Then he stepped forward.

"I think we have the man you want. You know that Louis Fleischner is a colonel in the Oregon militia. I'm convinced he is not the man to run away from Plummer. If he sees fit to accept, we can find none better."

Several dozen eyes turned toward the embarrassed hero of the Rogue War.

"Colonel, you lead us, and we'll all be with you," shouted the editor, who fancied himself the town's leading intellectual. Then turning to the whole crowd he asked, "What d'you say, men?"

There was a general outburst of approval. Everybody felt relieved now that a solution had been found.

"Here we go again," was Louis' resigned comment. "If it's not selling, it's soldiering, and I don't like either of these callings particularly."

"Do you accept?" asked Lewiston's self-appointed mouthpiece impatiently.

"All right, I'll lead the vigilantes, if only to show Plummer that not all men fade into corners when he walks by. Now, I count on everyone's full support if we are to accomplish anything."

"When do we have the first meeting?" another Blue Ox patron, a young blacksmith, wanted to know.

"What's wrong with tonight?" asked the new commander. "The sooner we get going, the less chance we give the Plummer gang to catch their breath."

"Wait a minute," whispered Julius into his ear. "Not tonight."

"Excuse me a moment, gentlemen," said Louis and, walking away a few steps with his partner, he inquired, "Why not tonight?"

"Have you forgotten our congregation?"

"No, of course not. But this is no Sabbath or holiday."

"No, but Solomon Frank has *yahrzeit* after his father. You know it's our unwritten rule to have a *minyan* for every Jew who wants to commemorate the anniversary of a family death."

"It had slipped my mind completely. We ought to

attend, or there may not be ten men for the *minyan*. You never know how many are out in the mines or traveling in the woods. Plummer 'll wait another day."

Plummer waited quite a few days. As soon as he got wind of the determined efforts to form a vigilante force, he decided to lay low. As if by magic, he and his henchmen disappeared from town. But nobody in Lewiston doubted that they were only biding their time.

When the twilight began to color the mountain slopes orange and purple, a dozen men assembled in the same shed in which Julius and Louis had earlier prepared their next pack trip. Bales and barrels had been pushed into corners. The floor was swept clean. By twos and threes the Jews who happened to be in the area drifted in. They nodded greetings to each other and then spoke about their recent mining luck and their plans for the next months.

This was a typical mining congregation. Similar groups could be found in California, Oregon, Idaho and Montana, wherever the precious metal attracted large numbers of seekers. Their sanctuaries were tents, rough-hewn cabins or just clearings in the woods. Nobody bothered with officers and dues. But when Passover or the Feast of Weeks came around, somebody was always found to conduct the service. If he did not have a rabbi's wisdom or a

cantor's silken voice, it did not matter too much.
The congregation was easy to please and there was
not much competition for these honors. When a
yahrzeit date was announced, everybody, even total
strangers, tried to attend the *minyan*. Often that
meant a hike of many hours.

Mining congregations existed one year or two,
sometimes only a few months. Then they dissolved
as the fortune-seekers moved on to more promising
claims. Bustling camps turned into ghost towns, and
the improvised synagogues lapsed back into silence.

But on this night in 1863, Lewiston's mining congregation was very much alive. When all were assembled, Julius Loewenberg stepped forward to
lead the prayers. Among those present, he was
by far the most learned in matters of religion. He
turned eastward and while the noise of merrymak-
ers from the Blue Ox filtered through the thin walls,
he solemnly intoned:

"Praise ye the Lord to Whom all praise is due.
Praised be the Lord to Whom all praise is due for
ever and ever—"

Some of the assembled who were familiar with the
ritual joined in the chants while others listened in
silence. Their minds wandered back to days long
gone by when they had attended services in duly
consecrated synagogues, in the company of Father or
Grandfather.

Now, at a sign from Julius, Solomon Frank began

to recite the words with which Jews everywhere remember their departed loved ones:

"*Yisgadal v'yiskadash sh'mei raboh*— Extolled and hallowed be the name of God throughout the world which He had created according to His will—"

After the service Solomon shook hands with everybody, thanking them for having come to make this event possible.

It did not take long till the talk shifted from matters of Jewish interest to the recent events in Lewiston. Everybody was deeply concerned.

One of the Jewish miners was bursting with the news of the most recent outrage, which had occurred some distance away from town. He was Sol Hirsch, a native of Poznan, a formerly Polish city, now held by the Prussians. Only this morning he and several companions had returned from the gold fields. Not far from the place where the Reverend Spalding once built his mission, the party was held up by three masked riders. At gunpoint they relieved everybody of his bag of gold dust and then hastily galloped off downriver.

Louis Fleischner felt called upon to look further into the matter. The importance of his new office had begun to impress itself on him. "Did you recognize any of the voices?" he asked.

"They tried to disguise them, had neckerchiefs tied over their faces as masks. All we heard was a low mumbling. But even so I'm quite sure that one of them was a man called Slim Parks. He worked with me for a time till he made off with some of my gear. Later I found out he had paid a gambling debt with it."

"Old Slim! Now he's become a highwayman. In a way I was fond of the rascal. If he could only 've stayed away from the dice. I feel truly sorry for him."

"Louis, don't you think we should do something about this holdup?" asked Julius.

"Certainly. They're only small fry compared to Henry Plummer. But if we act quickly it'll serve notice on all the outlaws in the neighborhood that their occupation has become extremely hazardous."

"You mean we can still catch those three?"

"There's a possibility. The trio is probably on its way to Fort Walla Walla. That is the nearest place where dust can be exchanged for currency and where goods can be bought. They will pose as honest prospectors who have made a big strike. What they want is to cash in all their loot before the news of the robbery gets to Walla Walla."

"Perhaps we can overtake 'em," said Sol Hirsch.

"I think we can. Their horses are tired, and their baggage is heavy. If we ride light, we may easily round them up before they reach the fort."

Julius was full of eagerness. "You're the commander of the vigilantes," he shouted. "Why don't you put your men to the test? At least you'll soon find out who's serious about curbing the bandits and who was only talking big this morning."

"You want a test? Well, here we go. A dozen of us are now assembled in this room. If we leave right away and everyone calls on at least three other men, we can mobilize practically the whole town. Ask the people if they feel this is important enough to lose a couple nights of sleep and a few days of work. If they can handle a gun and ride a horse, they should be at this place tomorrow at daybreak. We need provisions for one week, at the most. Good night now, and on with the work."

"I've never had such a *yahrzeit*," sighed Solomon Frank. "Let's hope next year it'll be a little less exciting."

2

Slim was entertaining his companions with funny stories as they rode along the Snake.

"That Hirsch fellow," he bragged. "The gun I pointed at his chest was his own. Stole it from him only last week. Should've said hello to it, as you do to an old acquaintance."

They laughed uproariously.

Slim continued: "I always like to watch their faces when we jump 'em. Some have such a stupid

look. Too bad I'm not an artist, or I'd love to paint
'em."

When the others grew tired of Slim's babbling,
they broke into a song. It was more like a Sunday
outing than a getaway after a crime, so sure were
the robbers that no danger threatened them. They
knew how reluctant miners were to leave their
claims and to bring reprisals upon their heads.
They also counted on the effects of Henry Plummer's reign of terror in and around Lewiston.

So they rode at a moderate clip. At night they
slept by an open campfire, not even bothering to
post guards.

Slim and his partners would have been less cheerful had they known about that other group that was
slowly closing in behind them. Those thirty men
rode in silence. They had no breath left for jokes
and songs.

It was on the second night after the *yahrzeit* service when the vigilantes caught up with their prey.
The glow of the fire could be seen from afar. Louis
and his men slipped from their horses and crept
forward noiselessly. They fanned out and ap-
proached the sleepers from all sides. It turned out
that the precautions had been unnecessary. The
three slept peacefully until their captors almost
stepped on them. Still groggy with sleep, the bandits found themselves securely tied with stout
ropes. Hands behind their backs, propped up in a

sitting position against a large boulder, they stared wide-eyed into the barrels of a dozen guns.

It took a while till they fully understood how serious their situation was. The faces of their pursuers promised no mercy. Their eyes were grim and hard. One of the thieves tried to wriggle away into the safety of the dark trees behind him. But with hands and feet tightly bound, he fell flat on his face and just lay there.

The bandit next to him, the one whose tenor voice had led the singing, began to beg for mercy. He promised to reveal the location of secret caches where they had hidden the loot of previous robberies. He offered to put the vigilantes on the trail of Plummer himself, though he probably knew no more about his whereabouts than did the people from Lewiston.

Slim, his black hair filthier and more matted than ever, looked from one face to another searching for a sign of compassion. With joyful surprise he recognized Louis.

"Co'nel! Boy, am I glad to see you! You still know me, don't you? I'm Slim, your travel pa'dner. You won't let those gen'l'men harm me, will you? You'll stand by me for old times' sake."

"Slim, I don't want to see you suffer, but this is out of my hands now. I've given you more than one chance."

"I know, I know. You staked me to gear and

grub when I was down and out. Several times you helped me in the mines when I was broke. But it's this cussed gambling. As soon as I see a pair of dice, I can't keep my fingers off 'em."

"Poor fellow, you picked the worst possible moment for that holdup."

"Hadn't eaten for three days. And believe me, the other two wanted to kill the miners. I insisted that we only take the gold—"

"Enough of this talk," broke in a deep voice with a broad drawl. It was Ben Duke, a powerfully built prospector from Dixieland. "Let's get this nasty business over with. The lowest limb on that tree looks strong enough. It'll hold all three of 'em. I'll be glad to string 'em up, and then we'll head for home. We've lost too much time already."

"No, sir." Louis Fleischner stood between Ben and the shivering captives. "There will be no hanging unless a court decides so."

There was tense silence for a moment over the nightly scene. The vigilantes crowded in behind Ben. Louis remained all alone between the two unlike groups.

"We've no time for courts and such fancy things," rasped Ben. "These leeches must hang."

Several voices shouted support for Ben. Impatiently the posse moved in closer. The space between them and their commander narrowed.

"Listen, men." Fleischner's voice was deadly serious. "I came to this country because it stands for fairness and justice. I want to keep it that way. You called on me to lead the vigilantes. I consented. I'm doing my part. Now do yours and obey orders like a disciplined body of men. You know very well that my orders are just."

He paused and looked them over, face after face. There was not a sound.

"These prisoners," he continued, "will be taken to Lewiston and tried in a court of citizens. We have no sheriff and no courthouse yet, but we know the spirit of the law. We know that every person has the right to his day in court. If these three are guilty they will not escape punishment. But I will not be a party to murder. That's what it would amount to. Now put them on their horses, take them in the middle, and let's be on our way."

A faint grumbling arose from the tight knot of human beings. But immediately movement came into it. Some went hastily over to the spot where the saddlebags were lying. It did not take them long to find all the articles the holdup men had acquired at their last ill-fated job. Others jerked the criminals roughly into a standing position and half lifted, half pushed them into the saddles of their horses.

The appeal to fairness and the strength of a voice skilled in giving commands had won out.

Ahead of the main body hurried a fast rider to carry the good news to Lewiston. When the strange procession came in sight, the whole town was out to welcome it. Commander Fleischner rode in the lead followed by three pairs of riders, each pair flanking one of the prisoners. The remainder of the force brought up the rear.

Triumphantly the throng moved down to the waterfront. Even the saloons were now empty, and their proprietors had no objection when youngsters carried the benches out and set them up by the boat dock. They were quickly filled with excited residents. Others stood behind the benches. A few armed men surrounded the prisoners, who had been taken from their horses. The guards were needed more to protect the criminals from the people than to prevent them from escaping.

"Let's start the meeting," shouted one impatient onlooker.

"Will somebody be the chairman," sounded off another.

Immediately the editor rose and stepped to the front. Ceremoniously he wiped his gold-rimmed spectacles on a silken handkerchief and put them on his protruding nose.

"Will the meeting come to order," he intoned. "In the absence of a permanent court we shall constitute ourselves as a court of justice. A jury of twelve is to be selected, and we must also choose a person of good reputation and upright standing to act as the judge."

"I nominate Colonel Fleischner for judge," drawled a deep voice. It was the same Ben Duke who had earlier favored a quick lynching. On the ride home he had thought the matter over carefully. The more he thought, the more arguments he found in favor of the orderly process of justice, though it took a little longer.

The nomination received several seconds and a general round of applause. Louis stood up to face the assembly:

"Thanks, folks, for your confidence, but I'd rather not accept—"

A murmur of disappointment swept through the rows.

"It's your duty," grumbled Ben, with a hurt look in his leathery face. "You're the one who always reminds us of our obligations in a democracy. A citizen has to bow to the will of the people."

Louis waited patiently for complete silence.

"I know about a citizen's duty. When you called on me to help in the fight against the outlaws, I gladly did my share though the work was not to my liking. Now, to act as the judge in this case is an entirely different task. I'm sure you wouldn't like the way I would handle it."

"What d'you mean?" inquired Ben.

"Many years ago, when I was a boy, I learned the saying,

'What doth the Lord require of thee
But to do justly, to love mercy,
And to walk humbly with thy God?'

You see, folks, I'm for justice the same as you, but I also love mercy. You will never convince me that a few bags of gold are worth the lives of three men. There is hardly any doubt how this trial will end. I know the verdict will be fair no matter who the judge is. But I'm not the man to send three other human beings to their death."

He turned to go. Then, as an afterthought, he added:

"Besides, my partner and I must start on our pack trip immediately. We've already delayed too long. Lots of hungry prospectors are waiting for us at Orofino. So long. I don't think Plummer or any of the others will bother you for a while."

The crowd was still silently mulling over the little speech when the two friends slipped away into the shed. During the next hours they were extremely busy. The goods had to be arranged into loads of four hundred pounds each. That was as much as one pack animal could carry. Then the fifty mules and twenty burros were lined up behind the building. The burdens were carefully wrapped and lifted on the backs of the animals. Each load was securely tied down with a diamond cinch knot. When the caravan was ready, the partners checked their guns and ammunition. Letters, papers and magazines addressed to the miners were put into waterproof pouches. Finally they saddled their own horses. Julius took the lead and Louis the rear.

They had worked through most of the night. Dawn was near when the long line began to move. An old gnarled tree stood at the edge of the little settlement. As the travelers passed it, they saw three silent figures hanging from its stoutest branch.

✞✞✞✞✞ *Lonely men*

The sun stood low over Orofino. It had been a scorching day, but now a cool wind was blowing through the canyon. Shaded by tall trees, the creek rushed along.

In the mining camp the long working day was about to come to an end. The last pan was filled with dripping creek sand. Then the monotonous rocking began once more, separating the heavier gold particles from the worthless material. The whipsaw cut the last log into boards that were needed for the trough-like sluice boxes. Tired fingers carefully poured the day's yield of gold dust into stout buckskin bags that were half filled with quicksilver. The heavy bags were securely tied and then hidden away till they could be sent to the assayer's office.

Their feet dragging from weariness, the men made their way to the hastily built lean-tos and tents they called home. Some started cooking supper on open fires. Others, their provisions gone, waited around for an invitation from a more fortunate neighbor.

Jim Pratt's cabin stood on a slope where most of the trees had been cut away for lumber and firewood. It overlooked a long stretch of the valley. While the brownish stew was bubbling in his iron kettle, Jim leaned against the doorpost looking out over the forest. The shadows were deepening. Suddenly he saw movement among the trees down by the bank. Now a man on horseback rode slowly out into the clearing followed by a seemingly endless string of gray animals. The bundles on their backs looked like grotesquely shaped humps.

"The pack train," shouted Jim. Still clutching the dripping spoon in his hand, he rushed down in long strides. Rapidly the word spread through the camp. The slope was alive with running figures. When the packers reached the first tents, the whole population of Orofino was assembled to greet them. The long-expected moment was here. Supper could wait.

Everybody helped willingly to unload the mules. The packs were arranged in straight rows and the patient animals turned out to pasture among the tree stumps. Then came the mail call. The leather pouch contained only a dozen letters or so, and they were at least half a year old. But the proud receivers wiped their fingers on their pants before taking them. They carried the wrinkled messages as if they were fragile treasures, though most of them could not read the contents. Later they would confidentially ask the packers to interpret.

Quickly the sale of supplies got under way. Prices were steep: flour sold at one dollar a pound; axes, saws and other tools were almost worth their weight in gold dust. Several prospectors were handed certificates showing that the packers had deposited their gold in the vaults of a bank.

The dying cookfires were stirred up again. Supper became now a holiday meal. Julius and Louis had to be very diplomatic because they did not want to offend all those who invited them to be their guests.

Afterward more than one hundred men sat around a huge campfire listening eagerly as Louis Fleischner read to them from newspapers and magazines many weeks old. Most of the news was about the Civil War which was now drawing into its third year. Jim Pratt, who had grown up in the Blue Ridge Mountains of North Carolina, beamed with pride as he savored the description of General Robert E. Lee's victorious march across the Potomac. But his face fell when the next antiquated news story reported the defeat of the Confederate Army at the battle of Gettysburg.

"Say, Co'nel," he drawled, unable to contain his disappointment any longer, "can you take some bags of dust out for me and see that General Lee gets them? I bet all he needs is a little more money, and he'll beat the pants off those damn Yankees yet."

"Look at Jim," shouted a fleshy-nosed New Yorker. "Why don't you take it home yourself to your plantation? Think of all the mint julep you're missing out here."

There was another round of laughter. Most Orofino prospectors were staunch Union sympathizers but, beyond some good-natured ribbing, no enmity arose with the few southerners in the camp. The bloody clash was too far away. Life in the mines was hard. The task of survival took up all energy. Yet when the strikes were good, the men wanted to support their favorite party back East.

The New Yorker was speaking again:

"Colonel, listen to this. I'll show you that we northerners can do more than talk. For every bag this cotton-picker here sends to the Confederacy, I give you two to deliver to the Union Army."

The boast was greeted with a general huzzah. Soon the packers were busy receiving pledges of gold in behalf of both the Blue and the Gray. A share of the wealth taken from the rocks of Idaho went to finance the armies of Americans fighting each other in Maryland and in the Mississippi Valley.

"Now, Jim," said the New Yorker, giving the tousle-haired North Carolinian a hearty slap on the back. "We've done our duty to the folks back home. Let's sit down and enjoy ourselves. Here, have a slice of my venison."

"Thanks, Chuck, you old rascal. If you weren't a Yankee, you'd almost be human."

"Colonel," asked Chuck, while his teeth were still chewing big bites of meat, "what do the papers say about fresh gold strikes? Rumors 're flying around that south from here, at Camas Prairie, a new rush is on. What's all this about?"

The eager faces around the fire showed that this was a topic of much more interest than politics.

Louis could not possibly read to them all the more recent articles about gold findings. He knew the contents already and so he summed them up in his own words:

"Yes, they're moving south in droves across White Bird Pass. The reports say that miners are also beginning to dig around the Boise area, and I've read stories about rich veins up in Montana."

They were all hanging on his lips. Fair amounts of gold were still being washed from the sands of Orofino, yet every rumor of paydirt found in other places made these people's spines tingle. They whispered into each other's ears. Questioning glances were exchanged.

As the fire burned low and all the questions were answered, the miners wandered off to their shelters. Exhausted from the day's travel and from the last hectic hours, Louis and Julius bedded down near what was left of their stores.

As Julius rolled himself into his blanket, he said:

"Prospectors are funny characters. They cannot stay long in one place. Did you watch their faces when you told them about Boise and Montana? The days of Orofino are numbered. In a few months this will be another ghost town. Are you thinking of moving on too?"

"No, Julius. This is as far as I go."

"But Louis, what's become of your hankering for new places? Are you getting old?"

"Chasing after gold from place to place has no future. What's the end of it? The richer the strike, the more you feel you've missed an even richer one. The miner is a doomed man."

"I see what you mean. The miners open up the country. But in ten or twenty years they'll be gone. The land will belong to the farmer and the stockman. And there'll be merchants and scholars in the new cities."

"Miners are after something. But that's not the

whole story. Often they're also running away from something."

Julius shot a glance sideways at his friend.

"You can only run away so far."

"Right, Julius. I'm beginning to see it. All my adventures have been a flight, you know from what. But this doesn't lead anywhere. There comes a time when a man has to stop grieving about himself and lend a hand to some worthwhile task, something that is sound and lasting."

"These are fine words, my friend. I'm very happy to hear them. Only one thing bothers me: what about our partnership?"

"I'm not running out on you just like that. We'll go back to Lewiston together, and we better start out soon. The animals cannot find much pasture here."

"And after we reach Lewiston?"

"Something's to be done about the gold. We never had such a heavy load to take out. All this generosity in behalf of Union and Confederacy."

"What're you planning to do with the gold?"

"It wouldn't be safe in Lewiston, not even in Walla Walla. I think I'll get me a good horse and ride on to Portland. It's the only place where I can deposit it without too much risk."

"Will you be back?"

"Probably not."

"I thought so. You seem ready to settle down and become a community builder."

"Why don't you come along, Julius?"

"Later perhaps. For a while I'll stay out here. These people need me, and it's good business though a little on the dangerous side. But don't be too surprised if I look you up in Portland some day."

"It will be a happy day for me. Whatever I have will be yours to use, Julius."

2

The pack train made good time on its return trip. Burros and mules were only lightly loaded, and the trail led mostly downhill. The caravan followed the winding creek through dense stands of pine and over outcroppings of rock high above the water.

More caution than ever was needed. Some slopes were too steep even for the sure-footed animals. They had to be unloaded, coaxed over the slippery rock, and then loaded again. It took time and patience to cross and recross the Clearwater. A hoof caught between boulders in the ice-cold water usually meant a broken leg and a bullet was the only remedy.

But the greatest danger was from human beings.

Louis Fleischner was a marked man for the outlaws. Henry Plummer had not forgotten the "Jewish gentleman's" defiance in Lewiston nor his swift capture of Slim's gang.

A change had come over the people of Idaho. Settlers and miners had lost their fear. No longer could the cutthroats swagger through the streets boasting of their crimes. Plummer knew he would have to do something drastic to get back into the saddle or else clear out of this part of the country. A daring raid, preferably one on the colonel's pack train, would give him just the kind of boost he needed.

Louis and Julius slept with their guns in reach. During the day they tried to shorten the line of pack animals as much as possible. They kept a close lookout, but one could not see far in the forest.

Then it came. Julius was in the lead. He had just left a gaily flowering meadow, and his horse was trotting between the creek bed and a tremendous overhanging boulder. His eyes were roving over the water in search of a good fording place.

Suddenly, high up on the boulder stood six men, guns leveled at the rider. They had not been there a moment ago. With legs planted apart, they stood as if conjured up by a magic wand. Their faces were masked. A voice snarled:

"Drop the gold bags right where you are and move on. Don't look back. Make it quick if you know what's good for you. If you play it our way, we may let you get away. We were not looking for you particularly."

Julius stared straight into the rifle barrels. He unfastened the thongs by which the bags were tied to each side of the saddle, and they slid to the ground. But at the same moment he gave the surprised horse the spurs. Cruelly the iron teeth dug into the flesh. The tormented animal reared and let out a long drawn-out cry of pain.

That was the prearranged signal. Louis, at the tail end of the train, heard it. Without waiting to get into view, he let go with a salvo from his two six-shooters. It sounded like a whole regiment practicing on the firing range. Since Louis was still hidden behind a bend of the trail, the outlaws could only believe that a strong escort was bringing up the rear.

The man who had stopped Julius led out a terrible curse. "The next time I'll finish you off, you Jew-packers. There won't be any challenge then, just bullets," he hissed. The rifle barrels were gone, and the sound of trotting horses faded into the distance.

Hastily Louis rode up to see what was going on. Julius wiped the sweat off his forehead as he tried to calm the panting horse.

"This was close," he gasped. "Why can't I find myself a nice, quiet occupation instead of dodging cougars and crooks by day and night?"

"Well, our little plan worked. Any idea who they were?"

"Not a shadow of a doubt. It was Plummer himself. I can recognize that poisonous voice anywhere."

"I thought so. My name leads his blacklist. But this'll finish him in the Clearwater Valley."

"I should say so. The miners 'll laugh him out of the Territory when they find out that we two beat off his whole band."

"Plummer 'll clear out from around here, but he'll probably take his business to Boise or Montana."

"In one of those places the tree's already standing from which he'll hang."

"Oh, that much is certain: he'll tie his own noose sooner or later. Now, Julius, let's get moving again. I see the excitement was too much for the mules. They're scattered all over. It'll take us several hours to round them up."

The two riders began to herd the frightened pack animals back into the clearing they had just left. The line was re-formed, and they moved on toward Lewiston.

3

The lone horseman urged the big brown mare to longer strides. He was riding westward, and the setting sun shone into his sunburned face. He did not mind because the rays were soft and caressing.

Horse and rider showed the effect of the long journey from Lewiston to Walla Walla and on to the Big Bend and farther through the Columbia Gorge. Louis had tried to avoid inns and settlements. It was better that nobody knew what he was carrying in his belt and in the bulging saddlebags. A large armed escort might have been advisable, but perhaps to be inconspicuous was the best protection under the circumstances.

Sleeping in the forest with the saddle as his pillow and cooking only sparse meals on tiny screened fires, he had made good time. On the whole, the trip had been uneventful and that was good. Any unusual occurrence could only have meant trouble. Now Louis was longing for the long-missed comforts of a hot bath and a soft bed.

Without stopping, he rode through the villages of Troutdale and Sandy. Only a narrow segment of the evening sun was still showing. Now he could see the houses of Portland in the distance. In front of them showed the masts of ships tied up in the Willamette River. How the town had grown in the last few years! The buildings were taller. Church spires reached out over the roof tops. The waste burners of several sawmills sent smoke and sparks skyward.

It was almost dark when he reached the east bank of the river that separated him from his goal. The landing was deserted, but the ferry could be seen rocking on the opposite side. Cupping his hands around his mouth, Louis let out a big shout. Nothing happened. He tried again. Finally, after he had almost shouted himself hoarse, the rickety boat began to move.

The old man at the tiller was in a bad mood. This was way past his usual quitting time. He felt that no decent citizen had any business crossing the river after sunset.

"Get your horse on board," he grumbled in a hostile voice. "Make it quick. I want t' get home. Fare must be paid on this side."

But his eyes bulged and his mouth gaped when Louis unloosened one of several small bags he had tied to his belt. It was bulky, and its contents glistened brightly as he opened it.

"I'm out of coins," said Louis. "Here, take some dust. I'm sure you won't have the worst of the bargain."

The sour expression quickly disappeared from the ferryman's face. This was worth at least twice the usual fare for man and horse. His toothless gums showed as he forced himself to a grin. Clumsily he tried to strike up a conversation:

"You sure struck it rich, stranger. Now you'll have yourself a wild time in Portland, I suppose."

Louis did not like the expression in the beady eyes.

"I hardly think so. Most of the gold isn't mine. It was given me in trust. I better get rid of it before the story makes the rounds."

The man at the tiller did not say anything, but his mouth made clucking noises.

"Tell me," asked Louis. "Where can I find a good, honest assayer?"

"Most of 'em are a bunch of thieves, if you ask me. I would take the bags straight to Bernard Goldsmith, the jeweler. And don't stop first in the saloons on First Street."

"No need to tell me that. Bernard Goldsmith, you say? Thanks for the advice."

"Yes, he'll treat you right. He's a Jew, but a fine man if there ever was one. A young fellow still and sits already on the city council. Has a good chance to be our next mayor. Well, here we are. Take it easy now. Ask for old Jeff if you need another ride across the river."

Louis was glad to be rid of the boatman. Quickly he left the dock. The fog gave the few forlorn street lamps a ghostlike appearance. Hardly a person was afoot. Louis stumbled along leading his horse by the checkrein. At long last he found the sign, BERNARD GOLDSMITH. ASSAYER AND JEWELER. GOLD BOUGHT AND STORED HERE. The small store was dark, but through the windows on the first floor shone light.

Louis knocked. There was no answer. The late

customer tried again, this time using his fist. After many more poundings, an upstairs window opened.

"Hey, you, what's the idea making so much noise at this hour?"

"I am sorry, Mr. Goldsmith, but I would like to deposit some gold dust."

The jeweler was surprised to hear himself addressed in such a polite manner. He had feared that the commotion was caused by some rowdy tippler. It wouldn't have been the first time in this waterfront town. His voice sounded much more pleasant when he asked:

"And why can't this wait till morning? Business hours are over, don't you know?"

"My name is Louis Fleischner, and I carry several thousand dollars' worth of gold on me. The gold comes straight from the Orofino mines. I hate to bother you, but it would be a great relief to me if I could get rid of my load this evening."

"You're Louis Fleischner? Why didn't you say so right away? Wait, I'll be right down. Of course, you're staying with us."

Soon the tired horse was stabled, and the buckskin bags were behind the heavy iron door of the strongbox. Louis was led into a cheerful room where the table was laid for supper.

"Emma," called the jeweler through the open door into the kitchen. "Imagine who's here: Louis Fleischner, Jacob's brother. Just arrived in Portland.

Get out another plate, and I'll open a bottle. This calls for a glass of Sabbath wine."

Emma Goldsmith rushed into the room, wiping her hands on the polka-dot apron. She was a pert, pleasingly plump woman with pink cheeks. Her brown eyes sparkled with kindness.

"Louis Fleischner, you say? Welcome home. We've heard so much about you. Wait till I tell Fannie."

"You can leave this for tomorrow," said her husband. "He's staying with us overnight."

Louis was puzzled.

"You talk about my brother and sister-in-law as if they lived next door. When did they come to Portland? Last time I saw them they were in Albany. I haven't had any letters from them for several years."

"Look at him. Doesn't even know about his own kin," bubbled the little housewife in mock anger. "Jacob and Fannie came about two years ago. You mean you don't know about your nephews either?"

"Nephews? I'm afraid not. Do I have nephews?"

"Now doesn't that beat everything? Has the two darlingest nephews and doesn't even know about them. Only this afternoon they were here with their mother visiting. I hope they like me half as much as they do my cinnamon cookies."

"So I'm an uncle now. Uncle Louis! Sounds strange. I'll have to get used to it."

"Now, Emma," broke in the host. "Do you realize

that this poor man must be starved? Hasn't had a decent meal for many days."

"Gracious, and me jabbering away here. Excuse me, men, we'll have something on the table in a minute."

She was gone, leaving an aroma of warmth and friendliness behind her. From the kitchen came the sound of clattering pans and tinkling glasses.

The two men sat down at the table. They had never met before, but after a short exchange of words they felt they had known each other for a long time. Louis learned, to his pleasant surprise, that Bernard Goldsmith shared with him many views and tastes. In more ways than one their experiences had been strikingly similar.

Bernard was also a veteran of several gold rushes. He too had done a lot of Indian fighting and attained officer's rank in the militia. Like Louis he felt, however, that the solution to the Indian problem lay not in better guns, but in honest cooperation and good will. Many times he had used his influence to prevent bloodshed and to make the white settlers understand the worries and suspicions of the roving aborigines.

"Yes, I've tried to follow your example," he told his guest.

"My example? But you didn't know me till an hour ago."

"People speak more often of you than you may

think. We admire your attitude toward the Indians and we try to learn from the way you gained their confidence."

"I'm happy I had a little success, but I had no well thought-out master plan. I only tried to do what my conscience dictated. All of us, the whole white race, carry a weight of guilt in this matter."

"You're so right. Emma and I feel very strongly about the unjust treatment of the red man."

"Emma and you—a real team of two. Bernard, you're a very lucky man. Emma is a great woman and a wonderful homemaker."

"Yes, we are truly happy. We were married in San Francisco only last year. I met her there when I first came out west on the Panama route. Then I moved on to the Oregon country while she stayed in the Bay City. Faithfully she waited for me till I was ready to come and take her with me."

Louis did not answer. His forehead rested in his cupped hand as he sat forlorn in thought. When he finally looked up, his face expressed not pain, but calm resignation.

Bernard remembered the story of his guest's disappointment. Jacob had once told him. Now he was sorry to have dwelt so much on his own happiness. To his great relief, Emma made her entrance at this moment, carrying an enormous tureen of soup.

"Ah, at last," he shouted. "We were about to stage a hunger riot and storm the kitchen."

"You've no reason to be impatient, Bernard. It's your usual dinner time. I was only trying to rush things on account of Mr. Fleischner. Well, here is your first meal in Portland. May there be many more."

Bernard broke the homemade bread which was still oven-warm, dipped a piece into the salt dish and gave thanks to the Creator:

"Praised be thou O Lord, our God, King of the Universe, Who bringeth forth bread from the earth."

It was a delicious meal from the soup to the fragrant *torte*, a baked dessert of German origin. A fire glowed in the stone fireplace. Everything, the white linen, the bright room, the gracious hosts, combined to make Louis feel warm and content.

Afterward Bernard and Emma tried their best to bring the wanderer up-to-date on his family and friends. They told him about Isaac and Marcus, his little nephews, and about the growth of the Portland congregation.

"You couldn't have come at a better hour," said Bernard. "Just in time for the holiday."

"Holiday? What holiday?"

"The first day of Succoth, of course. You must have lost track of the calendar out there in the wilderness."

"Yes, I did forget for a moment. I should've known better. On Yom Kippur I was completely alone. On a little hill overlooking the Columbia Gorge I fasted and prayed. There were no candles and no *shofar*. My father's prayerbook and prayer shawl which I had taken from the saddlebag were the only Jewish symbols around me."

"On the next Yom Kippur you will pray with us and, we hope, on many more to come. But first we must think of Succoth. It begins tomorrow evening. I'll be very happy to take you to the synagogue."

"Synagogue? Are they still holding services at Burke's Hall above the blacksmith shop?"

"Oh no, we have our own building now. It's only a small *shul* on Fifth Street, but it's ours. We feel at home there."

"Beth Israel has certainly made progress since I went away."

"Yes, we have almost outgrown the synagogue. It won't be long till we need a larger one."

"In the morning when we take you to Jacob's house," said Emma, "you can help your brother build the *succah*. Last year he had the prettiest in town."

"Jacob's quite an artist," added her husband. "Many of our Christian friends came to see it."

"Stop the chatting now, Bernard." Suddenly his little wife was very determined. "Don't you see how tired he is? Your bed is made, Mr. Fleischner. Bernard, you better show him now to the spare room."

The jeweler brought an oil lamp from the kitchen

and took his guest to the small room in the rear of the house. He put the light on the night stand. "Good night, Louis. May you find peace in this house and in this community."

Louis stretched out luxuriously under the soft down blanket. A new, immensely pleasant feeling enveloped him. The old wound had finally formed a healing scar. Here a new synagogue, a whole new society was growing. This was the end of the trail, a place where they could use some spare energy and enthusiasm.

🌳🌳🌳🌳🌳🌳 *Old memories*

Fifteen years had passed. Louis Fleischner was now forty-nine and one of the most respected residents of Portland. Whenever the full, ruddy face topped by the unruly mane of graying hair, was recognized on the street, people hailed him and stopped for a chat. He walked with a cane that had an ivory handle, as was the fashion in those days, but he was in the best of health and had no need of an artificial support. Talking on street corners with his many acquaintances, the simple people, as well as the pillars of the community, was his favorite pastime. He never tired of expounding his views on politics, the Indians, the future of the logging industry, or just the weather.

Louis was a wealthy businessman. The wholesale merchandising firm of which he was the senior partner was the largest and most prosperous of its kind north of San Francisco. Everybody who had any dealings with him admitted, often grudgingly, that this man with the gait of a woodsman had an uncanny talent in matters of finance. Nothing was too complicated for him to grasp, and he was always able to give quick advice to others who became lost in the tangle of interests, securities, and bonds.

Yet the work in offices and warehouses aroused only a mild interest in him. It was the bread-and-butter part, the least exciting phase of his life. But the progress of the community, that was a matter over which he could really get excited. Whether the project was to get a railroad built from Portland to Sacramento or to redecorate the New Market Theater, where the greatest artists of the time appeared, his name always figured among the prime movers.

The colonel was never content to be just a passive backer. To subscribe to a task meant for him to go out, roll up his sleeves and plunge right into the work. Louis loved to raise money, for others, that is, not for himself. It did not take long till he was looked upon as one of the leading philanthropists in the country.

Though the land of his birth had not been too kind to him, Louis, like many other Jews of the Northwest, retained a lifelong affection for European ways. He liked to read German, the language of his childhood. German books, German art and music always remained his favorites. Soon after moving to Portland, he became one of the chief workers in the local German Aid Society which looked after German-Americans who encountered rough going in the new country.

Then he was made president of the First Hebrew Benevolent Society. Early Jewish pioneers had founded it. There were no social security laws in those days and no welfare departments, but there were epidemics, accidents in the woods and sudden death in Indian wars. Frequent fires destroyed the wooden houses, and crop failures could bring long months of near-starvation in wintertime. The Hebrew Benevolent Society saw to it that Jews whom God had granted a measure of success shared some of their blessings with their less fortunate neighbors.

Louis spent less and less time with his own affairs and more and more with the problems of people who needed help. Under his leadership the benevolent societies of Portland developed into the best organizations of their kind far and wide.

There was one topic, however, which became an obsession with the colonel. No friend or chance acquaintance was safe from his long and sometimes tiresome speeches about it. His fond plan was to build a new synagogue for Beth Israel. Every time he went to services he pointed out to all who would listen how the streets around the *shul* were becoming shabbier and noisier. The synagogue was a plain frame building which seated, at the most, two hundred persons. A narrow, winding staircase, dark and slippery, led from the lobby to the women's balcony. On the high holidays and during memorial services the crowd was tightly packed, and the air was uncomfortably thick.

At first, the synagogue had seemed a great achievement to the pioneers, but now Louis felt the time had come to erect a bigger and better structure. On his trips to the East he had seen magnificent temples and churches. He had met architects, painters, and organ-builders. The more he saw, the more ambitious he became. Modesty had its place, but not where his synagogue was concerned. Faith of their depth needed, must have, a more fitting home.

The Jews of Portland smiled indulgently when he started on his pet subject. They tried to point out that, after all, Portland was such a young town and that its Jews numbered only a handful. The present *shul* would have to do for quite a long time yet. Why attempt the impossible?

But on the next Sabbath, walking home from the service, Louis would be at it again chiding them for their lack of vision. He was not prepared to give up.

"Sooner or later you will build the new synagogue," he liked to say, "if for no other reason, because you'll get sick and tired listening to me. But that's all right, as long as we get it built."

2

The spring of 1878 was beautiful in Portland. After
the long winter rains the air was clear and fragrant.
Mount Hood still carried its heavy coat of snow but,
in the orchards below, the blossoms of apple and
peach trees were a dainty white and pink. The roses
were beginning to bud, and from the open country
came the scent of ripening wheat and clover.

The Fleischner brothers, Louis and Jacob, were
sitting in a spacious room that looked out over the
westside hills. A large desk stood by the window. It
was of dark mahogany and matched the glass-en-
closed cabinets along the walls which contained
rows of stately volumes bound in red and gold
leather. Delicately designed damask tapestries covered the walls. Several large oil paintings in heavy
gilded frames were hanging on thick cords from
the moldings, and soft oriental carpets covered the
floor.

Louis rose and stepped to the window. The
house was surrounded by a park-like garden with
laurel and cedar hedges. Beyond stretched the forest. He waved to a group of three children seated
on little ponies. They were Isaac and Marcus, his
nephews, and Hattie, the oldest of his three nieces.

"Hi, Uncle Louis," shouted the children. Then they urged their tiny mounts and disappeared among the tall trees. An older man followed them on a slowly trotting horse. He used to be a miner, but the gold dust had run quickly through his fingers. Now he was grateful to the colonel for letting him look after the horses and watch over the children on their rides.

The house was one of the most beautiful residences in Portland. The wealthy bachelor had built it not for himself alone, but as the Fleischner family home. Uncle Louis was often gone on lengthy trips and he never returned without bringing presents for everybody, despite Fannie's faint protests that he was spoiling the children.

Louis looked in the direction where the children had disappeared. Hearing his brother's voice, he turned around.

"So you really want to go to Europe now?"

"This is as good a time as there'll ever be, Jake. Sol Hirsch and Alex Schlussel are very capable of looking after the business while I'm gone."

"You're lucky. Your business partners are still your friends. It doesn't always work out this way."

"I know. Even when I'm here, these men do most of the work. They don't seem to mind that I spend my time raising money for others."

"Why should they? As long as they come to you when important decisions must be made."

"During the next days I'll be very busy. I should like to leave right after Passover, and the holidays are only two weeks off."

"Is your itinerary made up?"

"More or less. I want to visit Italy and then go to Vienna. As a boy I always dreamed of seeing Vienna. On my list is a performance at the Imperial Opera House, a trip to the museums, and a stroll through the Vienna Woods. I read that Johann Strauss has taken the town by storm. I should love to see him conduct his waltzes."

"Sounds like a grand program. But you haven't forgotten a more serious duty?"

"You mean a visit to Vogelsang? No, I haven't forgotten."

"I feel bad that there's nobody to look after the graves of Father and Mother. All the relatives 've moved away."

"I'll take care of it. I also want to see Tachau and all the places where I spent my boyhood."

From outside came the sounds of clattering hoofs and rolling wheels.

"Now, who can that be?" muttered Jacob. "This is a most unusual time for visiting."

Through the window they saw a carriage and two horses enter the curved driveway. When the carriage drew up in front of the ivy-clad porch, the coachman stepped from his high seat and opened the door. Four gentlemen emerged, all dressed in ceremonial frock coats and high silk hats. Soon they could be heard coming up the wide stairway, and then there was a knock at the door of the library.

"Come in, gentlemen," boomed Louis' cheerful voice. A moment later he shouted, "Look who's here: His Honor, Mayor Goldsmith in person. And what d'you know? Is this a mayors' convention? Welcome, Mayor Friendly of Eugene? Sam, how've you been all these years? And what brings such an illustrious group into my humble abode?"

Bernard Goldsmith and Sam Friendly introduced the other two callers. One was a well-known member of the Oregon legislature and the other a personal assistant to the governor. Bernard acted as the spokesman:

"Louis, we come to you with a request. We represent a number of prominent citizens of both political parties."

"Sounds frightening. I hope I haven't done anything wrong."

"We are asking you to accept the nomination for state treasurer. You know in a few weeks we'll have the elections."

"State treasurer? You must be out of your minds. I'm just getting ready to go to Europe. Haven't been active in politics for ages. Get one of those ambitious young men."

Sam Friendly came to the help of his colleague:

"Look, Louis. We know that you have no ambition to hold public office. That's one of the reasons we come to you. The other is that the job we're asking you to do is extremely difficult and thankless. Oregon cannot afford a weak treasurer. The state finances are in a deplorable shape. Almost a million dollars have been loaned out in a very unbusinesslike way. I'm afraid much of it will never be collected. Nobody's ever bothered to set up rules for the handling of the treasury."

"Colonel, it looks bad," added the gentleman who represented the governor. "We fear the state might go bankrupt. That would set the development of the whole Northwest back many years. Who'd want to settle out here if we can't even run our government decently?"

"Still, I'm only a merchant, a private man."

"We all feel," said Bernard Goldsmith, "that you've just what it takes to get the state out of this mess. You don't need favors from anybody, and your honesty is beyond dispute. Just give the job a little of the zeal that made the Hebrew Benevolent Society so successful. That's all we ask, Louis."

"They could do with a little more energy and common sense up in Salem," admitted Louis. His mind was already working out solutions. Soon he was explaining to his visitors just what Oregon needed to get back on its feet. It did not take long and they were all crowded around his desk where he sat covering sheets with long columns of figures while giving a rapid-fire lecture at the same time.

"Which proves even more convincingly," said Mayor Goldsmith when Louis had to pause for a split second to gulp some air, "that we have found the right man. Do you have any of your delicious Purim wine left? Get it out, and we'll drink to the health of our next state treasurer."

Jacob had begun to open the cabinet where the ruby red liquid glowed in a cut crystal carafe.

"Wait a minute," cried Louis. "You're rushing me. I haven't accepted yet. And there's still the matter of the election."

"It's no use," said Jacob. "The old story again. You were sold on this job as soon as you heard how difficult and thankless it was. You'll take it. You'll work yourself ragged and you'll love it."

"But the election. Candidates have been defeated in elections before, as you know."

"Don't worry about the election," answered Sam Friendly. "There'll be no opposition. The Democrats want you, as well as the Republicans."

"Now may I fill your glasses, gentlemen?" asked Jacob.

There was no visit to Europe that spring. Louis Fleischner was elected by an overwhelming majority and moved to the capitol building in Salem.

3

It was four years later. Louis had just handed over the office to his successor and returned to the Fleischner home. This time nothing should prevent him from going to Europe. The trunks were brought down from the attic again to be filled with clothes and with presents for all the acquaintances of his youth.

While his sister-in-law was doing the packing for him, Louis sat in the library reading the morning edition of the *Oregonian*. A big headline on the front page proclaimed, COLONEL FLEISCHNER LEAVES STATE TREASURY. Underneath were his picture and two long columns full of praise. It said:

"—Colonel Fleischner did not seek the office of state treasurer four years ago. It was conferred upon him by the voters themselves, regardless of party lines or other groupings, because of his personal popularity and the confidence the people had in him. Now, as he returns to private life, all observers must admit that he was the best treasurer Oregon has had so far. He recovered for the state large sums of money that had been squandered.

He has introduced sound business methods in his department. His efforts have done a great deal to restore the people's faith in their state government—"

Louis put away the paper. Considerably more gray was showing in his mop of hair, and his cheeks were several shades paler than they had been four years ago. The outdoor complexion was gone. Only on rare occasions had he been able to sneak away for a day's hiking or horseback riding. Mostly he had sat chained to his desk in Salem, calculating, planning, and conferring with people from all walks of life.

But it was over now. In spite of all the difficulties, the haggling of selfish people, the stubborn opposition of many who resisted any kind of change, it had been a wonderful time, challenging and exciting.

With a sigh in which relief mingled with regret, the ex-treasurer rose to help his sister-in-law close the trunks. Tomorrow the stagecoach would take him to Sacramento. From there he had booked a place on the transcontinental railroad. It seemed only a short while since they had driven the ox team across the prairie. It took six months then, beset with hunger, cholera and Indian attacks. This time it would only be a few days.

4

Vogelsang was still a sleepy little town, and Jew Street was as narrow and crooked as ever. The houses looked even older now and they all were in need of painting and repairs. No iron chain barred the entrance any more, but the fountain still played in the middle of the street. Women came to fill their water jugs and stayed to chat a little. It was a welcome break in the long hours of housework.

On this morning, the women lingered longer by the fountain than usual. The visit of the rich American was an important event.

"Have you seen his carriage?" asked a young mother in whose arm a sleeping infant was cradled. "A Hapsburg archduke couldn't travel in anything finer."

Another woman stepped up to the water spout. But she was in no hurry to fill her bucket. "His pockets are bulging with presents. He's giving away silver coins as big as my palm."

"Look here, I have one." The proud owner held up a shiny silver dollar while the others clustered around to look and to envy. "Last evening he came to our flat. My David had gone to school with him. They talked about old times and what had become of all the boys of their class. When he left, he gave each child one of these coins."

"They must be worth a fortune," said the young mother.

"Yes, we're lucky. Sig Bloom, the pawnbroker, will give us ten Austrian *gulden* for each."

"And to think that I knew him when he was a little boy," chattered an old toothless woman. "If only his mother could've lived to see him. She was such a fine woman, but always so sad after her boys went away."

"Where's he now?" asked a matron who was struggling to keep a live chicken tucked under her arm.

"I saw his carriage about an hour ago," reported another young woman. "It stopped right over there at old Reb Sh'muel's place. The American went in. After a long time he and Reb Sh'muel came out together and drove away in the carriage."

"Reb Sh'muel went off in a carriage?" The old woman was very surprised. "He hasn't been out of his house for years. He's eighty-five, at least, and has the gout. Can hardly walk. He wouldn't have done it for anybody else. I wonder where they went."

"I can tell you," said a housewife who had just joined the group. Her large shopping bag was filled with fruit and greens. "They're down at the cemetery. I talked with the coachman. The American hired him in Prague."

On the edge of town, surrounded by a crumbling

stone wall, was the acre of land where the Jews of Vogelsang buried their dead. The carriage stood forlorn in the dusty road that lost itself in the farmland nearby. The coachman was napping on his seat, and the two matched bay horses munched oats out of nosebags that had been tied around their heads. Practically all the children of school age and below stood around watching.

The two men walked slowly along the narrow pathway. With one arm Louis supported his former teacher who hobbled with shuffling steps, depending heavily on his cane. A sparse white beard covered his chin, and the curled side locks below his black skullcap were thin and silvery. The eyes were the only part of his shriveled face that still seemed alive.

"Just take your time, Reb Sh'muel. I'm very grateful that you came out to show me the graves, but I reproach myself for having taken you away from your warm room."

"Don't fret on my account," croaked the old man in a shaky voice. "This is a great day for me. I haven't been of much use to anybody in the last years. All I could do was sit and study a page or two of the Talmud; then I would doze off."

"You have done your share of work in your days, and it's still well remembered. You were the best teacher I ever had. Do you know that it was mainly your inspiration that made me go to America?"

"God be praised for it. Often I sat by the fire and thought of you and Jacob. Your father and mother —may God bless their memory—came on Sabbath afternoons to show me your letters, and then we talked about you and your wonderful country."

"I should have come while they were still alive. I feel very guilty."

"You came as soon as you could. Your parents knew you had become an honest and successful Jew. They rejoiced that you lived in freedom and dignity. They died content."

"Still, I would feel better if I could have held their hands once more before they died."

"It was God's will, Levi—look. Over there, at the end of the path are the graves. I must stop and rest now. Walk on alone, and I will wait for you here."

Louis strode along past many narrow grass-covered mounds. The slender stones carried Hebrew and German inscriptions. On some could be seen two hands with fingers spread in the gesture of the priestly blessing. Others showed a water pitcher held over a basin.

The two unmarked graves lay side by side near the wall. Louis' head was bowed, and his thoughts wandered back to the last day at home. Again he was saying the morning prayers with his father. He could see his mother's tear-stained face as she kissed him goodbye.

Why had they not come to America? He had begged them often in his letters. But they did not want to be a burden to anybody, not even to their children. They were trees too old to be transplanted into foreign soil.

Reb Sh'muel was still standing on the same spot when Louis returned. With his humped back, the two bent legs, and the cane, he looked like a grotesque spider.

"I'm most thankful that you will see after the gravestones, Reb Sh'muel. I will leave an ample amount."

They began to walk back to the entrance. For a while nobody spoke. The former student's thoughts were still with the two graves behind them.

"Do you see this grave?" asked the old teacher, pointing with his cane at a mound of fresh, dark brown earth.

"Yes. What about it?"

"She was buried only last week."

"She? Who's she?"

"Hannah. You remember her, don't you?"

Hannah. Could he ever forget? So Hannah was dead, and he was standing by her grave.

"But Hannah lived in Prague," he said.

"She lived in Prague once. Then came the war with Prussia. Her husband lost all his wealth. He died a poor man. Hannah came back to Vogelsang with her children. Last year she took ill. Many months she lay abed in the house of her sister. When death finally came, it was a deliverance from suffering."

"In America sick people go to the hospital. Where's the nearest hospital around here?"

"In Tachau. But doctors and hospitals are not for poor people, my son. Remember, she was a widow, and she had growing children."

Hannah died poor and suffering. If he had only known. But how could he have known? Hannah was not part of his life any more. God's ways are sometimes hard to comprehend.

She was too poor to be cared for in a hospital. Don't poor people have a right to be cured from illness? Aren't their lives precious too?

A dull anger came over him. Perhaps in Europe nobody cared about such matters. People were born either poor or rich, important or unimportant, and that was that. But he was an American. Over there one felt differently about social injustice.

Louis thought of the large sum he had given to St. Vincent's Hospital, a few years ago, so that a room for poor patients could be equipped. Bohemia was not his home any more. Why should he be concerned with its sick people? And yet, what difference did it make? They were all human beings, suffering from the same diseases and needing the same cures.

He took the old teacher home, but refused his entreaties to come up and sit with him for a while. He promised to return the next day. Then he called, "Coachman, take me to the hospital in Tachau."

For two days the American visitor talked with doctors and city officials. He had lost all appetite for further travel. All at once he longed for the New World where people were concerned about each other's welfare.

Levi Fleischner departed, but he left something enduring behind. Soon after his visit to Tachau the usual quiet of the hospital grounds was broken by a swarm of workmen who began to saw and to nail. A new wing went up, reserved for the sick who were too poor to afford medical care. The bronze tablet at the entrance read, THIS WING WAS GIVEN BY LUDWIG FLEISCHNER OF PORTLAND IN THE UNITED STATES TO THE PEOPLE OF BOHEMIA.

The tablet did not say that the structure was also a memorial to a slim girl with golden hair.

✡✡✡✡✡✡ *How goodly are thy*

tents

Two men were placing chairs around a long table in the lobby of Beth Israel Synagogue on Fifth Street. An oil lamp with a tall smoke-blackened glass cylinder was suspended from the ceiling on a pull chain. It cast a dim light over a confusion of ledgers, notebooks and loose sheets of paper. Through an open door could be seen the darkened sanctuary. The pews stood in ghost-like rows. Without the worshippers they looked forlorn and naked. Only the Eternal Light in its bowl of red glass floated like a little island in the ocean of gloom.

Now the chairs were all in place. Sol Blumauer, president of the congregation, and Nathan Strauss, the secretary, sat down to go over the agenda before the meeting of the board of trustees was to begin.

The secretary was a little man with a high-pitched voice and nearsighted red eyes.

"We'll have the usual order of business, won't we?" he asked.

"I suppose so," answered Mr. Blumauer, a portly, white-bearded gentleman who was serving his tenth year as president. "Have you received any correspondence that should be read to the board?"

"Yes, Mr. Blumauer. Here is a letter from the chairman of the building committee."

"Oh, not again. Louis Fleischner is driving us all crazy. His trip to Europe was very restful—for us."

"But now he's back, and things are stirring again 'round here."

"Yes, he hit us like a hurricane. What does he want this time?"

"It's a short letter. He writes that the plans for the new synagogue are ready now. The architect has submitted his drawings. Mr. Fleischner found a Viennese artist whom we should commission to paint the frescoes on the inside. He's asking for the board's approval."

"Is that all? He just wants us to approve his grandiose plans. Has he also found a gold mine to pay for all this?"

"No, he doesn't mention any gold mine. But he says here that he will attend tonight's meeting and will be available for any questions the trustees might want to ask."

"Ah, he will be available. How nice of him. That means he'll talk us all to death again, and we won't get out of here till way past midnight."

"No use raving, Mr. Blumauer." The meek secretary sighed as he put the thick, yellowed record book in place. "You know as well as I do that it is hard to say no to the colonel."

"Well, I wasn't too serious. Just had to let off a little steam. Louis is a great fellow. We're all proud of him. His enthusiasm is like one of those new-fangled steam engines: it crushes and flattens every obstacle in its way."

"But it's also contagious like the sniffles in wintertime. We were all sort of lukewarm on the synagogue project till he came back and sparked things up."

"Yes, he gets things done. Now what else do we have on the agenda?"

Three hours later the air in the lobby was heavy with pipe smoke. The men sitting around the table were fighting with drowsiness. Some scribbled idly on the papers in front of them. Only the secretary's pen flew silently and evenly across the pages of the record book.

Louis Fleischner had unbuttoned his high-cut vest. The triangular tips of his stiff collar were drooping. Before him lay a confusion of drawings on heavy paper which curled into rolls and covered about half of the table.

His face was moist with perspiration as he unrolled a large sheet on which the outlines of a building had been sketched in regular lines.

"Look, gentlemen. The synagogue will be built in the Byzantine style. Here you see the broad frontal stairway. Ornamental wrought-iron lamp posts will flank it on both sides. Do you notice the twin towers above the main entrance? I'm sure they will soon be an outstanding landmark of Portland. We'll have tall, narrow windows filled with stained glass imported from Italy. As for the interior—"

He shuffled among the drawings till he found another roll covered with mysterious signs.

"The main hall will have a high, arched ceiling resting on two rows of pillars. The Ark and the organ front will be of Spanish cedar and maple. Incidentally, we should have the largest and most modern organ in the city. The pews will hold eight hundred people. In Vienna I met a very talented artist, still young, but with a great future. He is willing to come and paint the ceiling in fresco."

"And who's going to pay for all this?" groaned Sig Sichel, the vice president. "How much will it all cost anyway?"

"Seventy thousand dollars should pay for the building and the furnishings."

"Seventy thousand," exclaimed the vice president in anguish. "Do you realize that we have only one hundred and seventy families in our congregation?"

"Fortunately, Mr. Sichel, God has blessed several of us with considerable fortunes. I am sure all those gentlemen will be proud, as I am, to make substantial contributions so Portland can have a temple which will be a beautiful symbol of our religion and an ornament for the whole Northwest. May I have the honor of pledging the first thousand dollars, and I will also carry the costs of the frescoes."

"That takes care of the painter from Vienna," said President Blumauer with considerable relief. "The hour is getting late, gentlemen. Are you ready to adopt the plans?"

"What's the use voting?" grumbled Sig Sichel. "He always gets us around to where he wants us. We might as well have given him blank powers when we made him chairman of the building committee. As far as I'm concerned, if he can raise the money, he may have his Byzantine towers and his super-organ."

After the meeting the trustees came around, one by one, and wished Louis luck for the tremendous task he had taken upon himself. Once they were convinced that the goal was not completely out of reach, they were willing to submit to his leadership.

Those who still had their doubts gradually changed their minds during the next two years. Louis had practically resigned from his business duties. His days were spent buttonholing members and talking them into pledges double and more what they had originally intended. But curiously enough, afterward they all felt very good inside. He lost not a single friend during the campaign. On the contrary, he made many new ones.

Then came the day when ground was broken. The first scaffolds went up. Mortar was mixed in large flat troughs. Powerfully built work horses brought wagon upon wagon piled high with lumber. Slowly the architect's drawings were translated into brick, timber and glass.

The great moment arrived on a warm June evening in 1889. The corner of Twelfth and Main streets was jammed with people. Carriages were lined up at the curbs for many blocks. Sweating policemen kept open a path through the solid mass of curious onlookers who enviously watched the invited guests ascend the steps of the building.

City and state had sent their notables, and the leaders of many Jewish communities had traveled long distances to attend the consecration of Temple Beth Israel. The ladies looked dainty in their silk gowns with the narrow waists and the wide swooshing skirts. Their faces were shaded by huge hats on which artificial flowers, feathers and even whole stuffed birds reposed. Their escorts wore long frock coats and tall top hats. Many of the once rugged pioneers were now bent with age and had to be supported up the front steps by their younger kin.

Every pew in the sanctuary was filled. With awe

the crowd gazed at the silk hangings of the Ark and at the carved pulpit. Members and visitors tried to follow the impressive pattern of colors and lines on the ceiling. It was an intricate decorative design with an oriental flavor. Well-known Jewish symbols, such as the Star of David and the Menorah, stood out clearly. The light of countless candles and of many modern gas chandeliers cast a bright glow over the jubilant scene.

Now the first powerful chord welled up from the new organ. The music seemed to come from all directions at once, solemn, strong, and yet sweet. After a few cadenzas the sound of human voices joined in. High in the loft the choir intoned the ancient words of praise:

"How goodly are thy tents, O Jacob,
Thy dwelling places, O Israel!
As for me, in the abundance of Thy lovingkind-
  ness
Will I come into Thy house:
I will worship toward Thy holy temple
In the fear of Thee—"

The assembly rose to its feet, and all eyes turned to the rear entrance from where a procession began to make its way slowly down the center aisle. First came a group of visiting rabbis from congregations in California, Washington and British Columbia.

Behind them walked ministers of several Christian churches in colorful robes and cassocks. Then came the mayor of Portland and other high officials. The Reverend Jacob Bloch, cantor of Beth Israel, wore a white prayer shawl with blue stripes over his black robe and carried a gold-trimmed prayerbook. He was followed by the president and the trustees of the home congregation carrying Torah scrolls in their arms. The chairman of the building committee brought up the rear.

Louis was content with the minor role that had been assigned him this evening. Though he walked last in the procession, he felt it was his day of triumph. With a deep sense of fulfillment, he gazed upward to the ceiling and then around the spacious hall.

The Torah scroll he held was wrapped in a beautiful mantle of purple silk in which were imbedded gold threads and tiny stones of many colors. The crown, the frontal plate and the pointer were exquisitely hammered in silver and covered with graceful relief work. The scroll was several centuries old. It was the same copy from which he had once recited the weekly portion in the Vogelsang *shul*.

The thought had occurred to him on his trip to Europe when he visited the old prayer room where he had worshipped as a boy. He discussed it afterward with Reb Sh'muel. The venerable teacher

promised to take the matter up with the elders of the
shul. A very substantial gift to the poor of Jew
Street was to be part of the transaction. About a
year ago, shortly before his death, Reb Sh'muel
wrote that the scroll was on its way to America.

Louis' face was hot under the clumsy, stiff hat,
but he had no feeling of discomfort as he walked toward the platform. When he passed a corner pew,
he heard a man explain to his neighbor, "Here goes
the fellow who really built the synogogue."

Now the procession ascended the dais. The digni-
taries formed a semicircle around the open Ark. A
small girl dressed in white recited a little poem and
then handed the key to the synagogue on a pillow
to President Blumauer.

Then the oldest visiting rabbi kindled the Eternal Light in the ornate bronze bowl. With a tremor
in his voice, he chanted the *shehecheyonu.* Hearing
the words, Louis remembered a dusty rider on a
hilltop looking for the first time at the Columbia
River at his feet.

While the choir sang a triumphant anthem and
the organ gave it a warm, luxuriant background of
harmony, the Torah scrolls were deposited in the
Ark, one by one. From now on, the words written
on them were to inspire a group of Jews living as far
away from the homeland of the Bible as one could
possibly get.

The curtain with the embroidered likenesses of

the two Tablets of the Law was closed, and the crowd settled down to a long service punctuated by many speeches and hymns.

Afterward there was a smaller celebration in the living room of the Fleischner home. A few friends had come to congratulate the sixty-one-year-old fire-brand on the success of his greatest project. Bernard Goldsmith, the former mayor, was there, and so were Sol Blumauer and Sig Sichel, the two Jewish leaders who once had their doubts about the colonel's good judgment. Another well-wisher was Julius Loewenberg, now a Portland banker. With an iron grip he shook the hand of his former partner on the Idaho packing trips.

Fannie Fleischner was, as always, a gracious hostess. The whole family was present to honor Uncle Louis. There were Isaac and Marcus, already active in the family business, and the three girls who had just returned from boarding school. Beside Isaac sat a slender young lady of great charm, his bride of two months. After the couple had paid their respects to the famous uncle, they spent the rest of the evening gazing into each other's eyes, only dimly aware of what happened around them.

The hour was late, but the group was still in high spirits. Suddenly the doorbell sounded. Astonished Louis rose to see who the late caller might be. In the doorway stood a grizzled man, at least twenty years Louis' senior. His face had the color and the markings of old tree bark, and the bushy white mustache drooped over the ends of his mouth.

"So you don't know who I am, Colonel," cackled the stranger. "Had a date with you tonight and I kept it."

"A date? With me?" Louis thought the old man's mind had begun to slip. Or perhaps he mistook him for another person.

"Came all the way from Kalama," continued the late visitor. "I was sitting right there in that new church of yours, but you never saw me. Almost passed out. Too crowded for an old mountaineer."

The voice was vaguely familiar. Louis searched his memory. A date tonight at the consecration; calling the synagogue a church—which was only done by non-Jews—how did it all connect? Then there was a flash of recognition. An incident long, long forgotten came to his mind.

"Why, it's Ezra Meeker." Tenderly he placed his arm around the old trail guide's shoulders and led him into the house. "What have you been doing with yourself all the time?"

"Guided a few more parties over the Oregon Trail. But none gave me as much trouble as yours, what with all the sickness and Indian fighting. Then I got me a land claim and settled down on the Washington side of the river. Had a rough time clearing the land. Trees are mighty big there. Now the children and grandchildren 're taking care of the farm."

Most guests knew of the weathered old pioneer. Ezra Meeker had become a legend around the Oregon country, especially after the publication of his experiences as a mountain man and trail boss.

It took only a question or two, and Ezra was holding forth at length on his adventures in the early days. But in the midst of his reminiscing he checked himself:

"Listen, folks. I didn't come here tonight to sound off about myself, much as I like to. You want t'know why I came? Don't go much partyin' any more, particularly when I'm not invited." He cast a mischievous glance in the direction of his host. "But this is something special. I came to pay up on a bet I lost. It's a long time since we made that bet, over thirty-five years."

"Now I remember." Jacob turned to the guests and explained. "One night, on the Oregon Trail, he and my brother were arguing if Jews made good pioneers. Ezra didn't think Jews would ever come to the Northwest in any sizable number or, even less, stick it out after they came. He bet Louis a rifle that there'd never be enough of us to have a church of our own. Do I recall it right, Ezra?"

"Yep, that was the bet. And strange to say, I'm rather glad I lost it."

"Now you owe me a hunting rifle," laughed Louis. "Better make it one strong enough to shoot elk. I can use one."

"You think I would let down on my pledge? Don't insult me. The gun is outside the house right now, leaning against the door. Finest rifle you ever saw."

"Good boy. Why don't you come hunting with me? Let's try it out together. What d'you say?"

"No, thanks. Tomorrow I'm going back to Kalama. No more running around in the woods for me. My hunting days 're over."

"How did you find out about our new synagogue?" asked Jacob.

"I may be just a rough mountain man, but I've learned to read."

They all laughed, thinking of his fame as a writer.

"Couldn't miss it. It was all over the papers," he continued, "how Louis here worked his head off for this building. And I also found out that you've had a little church since 1858. That makes me a little late with my rifle."

"It's good you waited," said Jacob, "till Louis built us that fine large synagogue."

"No, I didn't build it. I could've never gotten anywhere if our people hadn't shown that go-getting pioneer spirit. All they needed was someone to stir them up a bit."

"You must've done a good job stirring." Meeker slapped his trail companion on the back. "It's one of the most beautiful buildings I ever saw, and I've been around the whole United States many times."

A moist film covered Louis' eyes. "It's what I learned from people like you, Ezra, on the Trail and out here, on America's last frontier, that enabled me to win our bet."

Young Isaac Fleischner looked thoughtfully at these men who had carved out new communities from the wilderness. The roughest part of the pioneering job was finished, but a lot still remained to be done. His eyes turned back to his lovely wife, and he reached for her hand. She squeezed his fingers as a sign of understanding and willingness. They would continue the task.

Covenant Books

Stories of Jewish Men and Women
To Inspire and Instruct Young People

Covenant Books are a new and fascinating series designed to take young people, eleven to fifteen years of age, on an adventurous expedition into the realms of Jewish experience. This is achieved by means of colorful biographies of Jewish personalities—prophets, rabbis, martyrs, philanthropists, writers, scientists—each representative of the many facets of a great tradition.

Covenant Books Already Published